VICTORY in DEFEAT

MEIANGELO TAYLOR

VICTORY *in* DEFEAT

Helping Father's and Men Restore Order Attitudes & Responsibility in Families

TATE PUBLISHING
AND ENTERPRISES, LLC

Victory in Defeat
Copyright © 2015 by MeiAngelo Taylor. All rights reserved.

No part of this publication may be reproduced, stored in a retrieval system or transmitted in any way by any means, electronic, mechanical, photocopy, recording or otherwise without the prior permission of the author except as provided by USA copyright law.

Scripture taken from the *New King James Version®*. Copyright © 1982 by Thomas Nelson, Inc. Used by permission. All rights reserved.

This book is designed to provide accurate and authoritative information with regard to the subject matter covered. This information is given with the understanding that neither the author nor Tate Publishing, LLC is engaged in rendering legal, professional advice. Since the details of your situation are fact dependent, you should additionally seek the services of a competent professional.

The opinions expressed by the author are not necessarily those of Tate Publishing, LLC.

Published by Tate Publishing & Enterprises, LLC
127 E. Trade Center Terrace | Mustang, Oklahoma 73064 USA
1.888.361.9473 | www.tatepublishing.com

Tate Publishing is committed to excellence in the publishing industry. The company reflects the philosophy established by the founders, based on Psalm 68:11,
"The Lord gave the word and great was the company of those who published it."

Book design copyright © 2015 by Tate Publishing, LLC. All rights reserved.
Cover design by Bill Francis Peralta
Interior design by Richell Balansag

Published in the United States of America

ISBN: 978-1-68187-471-5
1. Self-Help Motivational & Inspirational
2. Self-Help Personal Growth / General
15.09.18

A Creed for Success

First you have to dream about it!
Then think all day and night and have a *gleam* about it!
Be willing to die for it! Not ashamed to cry for it!

Tell the world about it!
And when they don't believe, not have any doubt about it!
You have to develop it, *perfect*, and relish it!

Be willing to freely share it!
That's how you *truly* prepare it!
You have to embrace it!
Not do anything to disgrace it!

You have to believe in it, in order to *achieve* in it!
Give your heart and soul for it!
Find all options to explore for it!

If you have great *persistence* and don't give in *to any resistance*!
Using all your strength and power, there are no walls or obstacles you cannot tower!
If you give your blood, sweat, and tears for it!
Surrender *all* your failures, fortunes, and fears for it!

If you are courageous for it!
Willing to follow all the steps and stages for it!
Then and only then will it be before you to grab it!
And with God's grace and mercy, you will surely have it—*success*!

Acknowledgments

First and foremost, I want to thank my Lord and Savior Jesus Christ for giving me the vision. I know without you, my life would be nothing. You have kept me during many storms in my life.

To my parents, Delores and Waverly, thank you for bringing me into this world and for all the life lessons you have taught me. No matter what life brings my way, you have always believed in me. I love and appreciate you for it.

To my big brother, Renaldo, I want to tell you thank you for being my guide. I have always looked up to you. Thanks for being there for me through tough times.

To my grandparents, Annie Pearl and Ezekiel, who are no longer with us, you all stepped up in the absence of my parents and really made a difference in my life! Your words of wisdom still ring true to this day. I miss you both tremendously.

To my wife, Latoria, without you, none of this would be possible. You came into my life and gave me confidence. Your belief in me gave me the strength to feel as though I could conquer all obstacles. Tori, you are my everything, and I love you unconditionally.

To my children—Imani, Marcus, Kyla, Tyler, and Mykaela—I love you all very much! Everything I do, I do so that you all know that anything is possible. My desire is that after you all see me chasing after my passion and purpose, you will decide to do the same in your own lives.

To my spiritual father, Apostle A. R. Williams of World Overcomer's Outreach Ministries, thank you! Thank you for teaching me the importance of finding purpose and destiny for life. Without your teaching, this would not have been possible. Thank you for being a great teacher and spiritual mentor, giving me an example of what a man, father, husband, and leader should be.

Contents

Introduction 11
Preface 19

Part I: Turning Boys to Men

1. Living on Purpose 27
2. Breaking Family Cycles 39
3. Check Yourself 53
4. Man Up! 63
5. Fatherless Landfills 73
6. Submission to Authority 83
7. Purpose for Work 97
8. Don't Be Lazy! 107
9. ROAR like a Lion! 113

Part II: Words of Love to My Wife and Children

10. For That Reason Alone, I Love You 125
11. What Your Love Has Done 129

Afterword 131
References 135

Introduction

Nothing I've ever done has given me more joy and rewards than being a father to my children. (Bill Cosby)

> **Interesting Fact**
>
> Children in father-absent homes are four times more likely to be poor. Children born to single mothers show higher levels of aggressive behavior than children born to married mothers. (US Census Bureau 2011; Osborne and McLanahan 2007)

I'm not ready! That was my first thought when I received a letter from my daughter Imani's mother, Gloria, telling me that she was pregnant. It was 1996, and I was in the Army stationed at Fort Campbell, Kentucky. For a very long time,

I refused to write or call Gloria because I was afraid, afraid because I had no idea of what it meant to be a father. I knew that I was not equipped with the necessary tools to be an effective parent. In my juvenile mind, I believed that perhaps if I didn't acknowledge the fact that Gloria was pregnant, then the pregnancy was not real, and I wouldn't have to take responsibility.

Several months later, my girlfriend at the time who would eventually become my first wife, Lynnette, said to me that she also was pregnant. Pregnant! I remained cool, calm, and under control with a simple reply of okay. She thought I was the best guy in the world because I kept my cool. On the outside, I might have been under control, but on the inside, I was living a nightmare.

For the record, let me paint the picture on how this all happened. In 1995, I graduated from Hamilton High School in Memphis, *Tennessee*. I had been dating a young lady named Reynada ever since the eighth grade. For four years, I assumed this would be the girl I would one day marry. Looking back, I don't know why I thought Reynada would have married me. I was physically and emotionally abusive. I thought that was the way to get a woman to listen and do what I wanted her to do. Thank God for maturity and growth as a man. I now know that my thinking and actions were wrong. As a man and a father of daughters, I now know it is wrong to be physically or emotionally abusive in any way.

This abusive relationship eventually took its toll on Reynada, and when she went off to college, we started to go in separate directions. That was when I began a strictly friendly relationship with my first daughter's mother, Gloria. Gloria had recently lost her mother to cancer, and I would go by her house and take her food or just check on her because she was depressed about the death of her mother. We would talk about life, where we wanted to be in the future, and occasionally, I would talk to her about my troubled relationship with Reynada.

One thing led to another, and before you know it, we are comforting each other during our difficult times. Unfortunately, when you are eighteen and seventeen and you are alone at home, the comforting can lead to other things. I told Gloria that would be leaving to go in the military in a couple of weeks. I asked her to join the military as well because I was concerned about her staying in Memphis by herself with her state of mind being so fragile in my opinion. She refused the invitation and decided to stay in Memphis. Gloria found out she was pregnant after I had already left for the military. Gloria and I were not in a relationship at the time; we were friends who had crossed the line and entered into a sexual relationship.

After being in boot camp for two months, I received the letter saying that Gloria was pregnant, and that I was the father. My initial reaction again was to avoid it and act like it was not real. I never replied to the letter because I was scared. Now I want to make a point here. Oftentimes, men will run from responsibility out of fear—the fear of failure, fear of the unknown, and fear of disappointment.

Not because we desire to be deadbeat dads, not because we don't love our children, not because we don't care, but simply because we are scared of the responsibility.

I went on for the next few months as if I never received the letter from Gloria and continued to live my life and made bad decisions. After basic training, I was permanently assigned to 101st Airborne Division Air Assault. There I met Lynnette who was from New Jersey. We began hanging out and dated for a brief time, and after a few months, I learned that she was pregnant as well. Keep in mind, I never told her about Gloria or the letter she had written me. Here I am now at nineteen years of age with two different women, pregnant at the same time, and neither of them knows about the other. I still continued to ignore Gloria's attempts to contact me about my child.

> **Interesting Fact**
>
> The largest geographic area of sustained fatherlessness contains the rural largely black poor across Arkansas, Mississippi, and Louisiana, Tributaries of broken homes running 400 miles along the Mississippi River from Memphis, *Tennessee*, where in some neighborhoods 82 percent of children live with their mothers alone. (Anderson 2013).

One Saturday afternoon, I was sitting in my barrack room when I heard a knock at the door, and it's Gloria. Sure enough, she was pregnant about eight and a half months by this time. When I let her in, I was nervous because my past had finally caught up with me. All the unanswered letters and phone calls had finally found its way to my doorstep. I was also nervous because my other pregnant girlfriend lived four doors down in the same barracks as me, and I was hoping that they would not cross paths.

I listened as Gloria chastised me for not returning her calls or letters. I tried to come up with a good excuse for my dismissive behavior; none of which Gloria was buying. Suddenly, I heard another knock at my room door. I tried to act as if I didn't hear it, but I couldn't, so I walked to the door. That was the longest walk of my life. My heart was racing like I had just finished the Boston Marathon. When I got to the door, my worst nightmare had been realized. It was Lynnette on the other side. I refused to open the door. I waited for her to leave and go back to her room. Later, I tried to sneak Gloria past Lynnette's room and out of the building; however, Lynnette saw this pregnant girl leave my room, and she was furious.

That evening, I finally broke down and told both Gloria and Lynnette about each other. That was the most stressful day of my life. I had to finally begin taking responsibility for my actions. It wasn't anyone else's fault; the fault fell squarely on my shoulders. My reckless and undisciplined behavior had gotten me to this point in my life, and now, I would have to make a decision on what I was going to do.

So early one morning, I sat in my barracks room, and I calculated in my small mind how I could make this all work out. I acknowledge that at nineteen, I didn't know much, but I did know that I wanted a relationship with my children. Growing up, my family structure was dysfunctional. My mother struggled with addiction, and my father struggled with mental illness. There was also a healthy dose of domestic violence in the middle. Because of this, I *always* had a desire to be a better parent for my own children someday. I just didn't plan on it starting like this.

So as I started thinking of how to make this work, I made a decision. My decision was to marry Lynnette, not because we were in love, but simply because of geography. Lynnette was from New Jersey and had planned on staying in the military and going to Germany. Gloria at this time had moved from Memphis to Nashville to attend Tennessee State University. My logic was if I allow Lynnette to leave, there is a possibility I won't get to see my child again. That was not something I wanted to have happened. I thought after college, Gloria would move back to Memphis, and both my children would be living in the same city so I could be a constant part of their lives. Gloria, however, decided to remain in the Nashville area, got married, and started her family there. Sometimes we can have a plan, but it never works out the way we think it will. That was the logic I used to get married seven months after meeting Lynnette. My life has taken me many places, and because of that, I believe God has destined me to write this book about fatherhood in America!

I believe that the only way to help others is to be transparent in your own life. I hope that this book can be just that. I am not proud of the mistakes that I have made in life, and there have been many. However, if my mistakes can help others overcome adversity, then it is all well worth it. I know that the trials we face in life are mere building blocks to get us to the place that God has designed specifically for us.

This book is about how our decisions help shape our lives, community, and world. It's about men finding purpose for their lives. It's about a life's journey to break family cycles. It's about learning to confront your past so you can have a successful future. It's about admitting fault and growing to become a better man, father, and person. It's about understanding that your children are your legacy, your most important investment on earth. It's about men understanding that *being present is the most precious, priceless, and perfect gift a father can give his child!*

I pray that my story will inspire men to step up and reconnect with their children and work on a lifelong relationship that develops love, respect, and trust!

Preface

Anyone who knows me knows that I am a diehard San Francisco 49ers fan. For eight years, they hadn't even sniffed the play-offs. A franchise that had gone twenty years winning at least ten games a year became a laughing stock. This once proud organization had become the doormat of the NFL. However, after years of mediocrity in 2011, something happened. The team hired Coach Jim Harbaugh, and they started winning again; and in his first year, he took the team to the NFC Championship game losing to the New York Giants in the final minutes of overtime.

The following year, the Forty Niners were one of the preseason favorites to represent the NFC in the Super Bowl. They started out the gate very well. However, midway through the season, the starting quarterback, Alex Smith, got hurt in the game against the St. Louis Rams; and the backup Colin Kaepernick, a second year player, took the starting job and never gave it back.

Kaepernick is a dynamic player who adds something special to the team that had been lacking since Steve Young was quarterback. He took the team through the season to win the NFC west with an 11-4-1 record. In the play-offs, the team took on the Green Bay Packers in the divisional round and won 45–31. In the conference finals, the team took on the Atlanta Falcons and won that game as well 28–24. Finally, after eighteen years, the team had finally made it back to the promise land the Super Bowl. The Super Bowl was to be the Baltimore Ravens vs. San Francisco 49ers in New Orleans at the Superdome.

The year 1994 was the last time the 49ers were in the Super Bowl, which was my senior year in high school. When they made their journey back to the big game in 2012, I immediately started making plans to travel to New Orleans to be a part of the action. I connected with two like-minded friends, and we planned the trip to head to New Orleans and partake in the Super Bowl activities.

We drove down from Memphis on a Friday morning and got a hotel room in Bay St. Louis, Mississippi. We all stayed in one room, and it didn't seem to matter because we were there in the midst of it all. We walked Bourbon Street in the day's leading up to the Super Bowl. Before the game, you could find us talking trash to the Baltimore Ravens fans about whose team was better.

After eighteen years of suffering, game day had arrived. We woke up early that morning with great expectation.

We got dressed and headed into New Orleans to the NFL Experience event. This was a fun field event that allowed people an opportunity to participate in mock drafts, interviews, and many other attractions. We had an amazing time, and I was even interviewed by a national writer for the Associated Press. Once we left the NFL Experience, we headed over to Harrah's Casino to watch the game.

When the game started, it went downhill fast! The halftime score was Ravens 21 49ers 6, and it should have been worse than that! After halftime, the ravens received the ball first, and Jacoby Jones proceeded to run the kickoff back for more than 100 yards. That took the lead to 28–6 Ravens. Then the infamous lights out incident happened, and we waited at least thirty minutes or more for the game to resume. Once the lights came back on, the 49ers made a feverish comeback, cutting the lead to 28–23 in the final minutes. The 49ers had the ball first and goal on the three-yard line. The 49ers could not score the game winning touchdown and ultimately lost the game 34–31.

When the game ended, I made a beeline to the car. I was upset and just didn't want to be bothered! On the way to the car, we ran into several Ravens fans who were excited in the street. One particular female fan ran up to me in excitement saying the 49ers were garbage. I look at that lady and said, "With all due respect, ma'am, now is not the time. Please get out of my face." And I continued to walk to the car.

The Eric Thomas Experience

When we got to the car, I was so upset I didn't say a word. I just laid down in the backseat and fell asleep. After about an hour of sleeping, I awoke to the voice, saying, "You have to want to be successful as bad as you want to breathe." Turns out, one of my friends had downloaded a gentleman by the name of Eric Thomas. Mr. Thomas is a motivational speaker who delivers a dynamic message with energy and enthusiasm. I sat up in the backseat and listened to every word that he was saying. He talked about how "in order to become successful, you can't take any days off." He was powerful. We listened to him the entire ride back to Memphis. He is the reason I titled this book *Victory in Defeat* because it was in defeat that I found strength. Strength to begin the process of finding my purpose for life. When we got back to Memphis, I watched all his motivational videos on YouTube and started to take action steps to become successful. I always knew that I had a story to tell; I just never really knew how to get started. I knew that I needed to become a better speaker, so I joined Toastmasters International. While involved with Toastmasters, I won several group-speaking competitions. Later, I entered a humorous speaking competition and made it to the division level before taking second place. One day, I hope to meet Mr. Thomas and thank him for helping change my life!

My wife, Latoria, and I started developing a name, mission, and vision for what would become the nonprofit organization Inspire "Growth Beyond Measures." I then developed a program designed to get fathers to reconnect to their children and called it Men ROAR—meaning Men Restoring, Order, Attitudes, and Responsibilities. From the creation of this program, I decided to write this book to share with men the important role fathers play in the lives of their children. The program is twelve weeks, and it teaches men that there is meaning and value in the father child relationship. The program also talks to men about the purpose for work, having a spirit of excellence, and many other topics.

What I found to be so wonderful was that in the midst of defeat, I have found happiness and joy because I now know what I am supposed to be doing with my life! No more aimlessly wondering around without any vision or goals in mind. I got it, and I get it now! I have found my victory in defeat! Sometimes it takes crazy circumstance to get you up and at them! I hope this book inspires men to chase their passion, turn their pain into their prize, and restore relationships that have been broken!

PART I

TURNING BOYS TO MEN

1

Living on Purpose

> That in all known societies, all male children have an acknowledged male parent. That's what we have found out everywhere… and well, maybe it's not true anymore. Human societies change. (Bronislaw Malinoski)

In the spring of 2002, my son Marcus has just turned five years old, and I decided that I wanted him to play little league football. One day, I stopped by the local football field where I saw children at practice, and I got information on when Marcus could come and tryout. I rush home excited because it has always been my dream to have my son play football. I thought the game would toughen him up, but honestly, I was attempting to live out my childhood fantasies through him.

Men oftentimes, without even thinking about it, unfairly place expectations on our children to live up to the failed dreams of our own lives. Like most men, I had a desire to play football professionally, but the truth of the matter is, I was not either good enough or disciplined enough to make that dream a reality. So my natural instinct at twenty-two was to try and make me son become something that I could not. Men must first know what their goals are before they can help their children find purpose!

List five goals you have as a man.

1. _____

2. _____

3. _____

4. _____

5. _____

When I got home, I walked in the house feeling like I was the best dad in the world. I truly believed that if I loved football, surely, he would as well. That's my boy! When I got to his room with the shoulder pads and helmet, I said, "Marcus, you gone play football this year. Are you excited?"

He looked up at me with skepticism in his eyes, and he said what any five-year-old who didn't want to disappoint his father would say. He said yes, but his body language told a completely different story. If I would have been in tune with him like I was supposed to, I would have known that he hated football and didn't understand why I would act so ridiculous whenever I watched it on television.

The next week after school, I helped Marcus get ready for practice. I remember putting the hip, thigh, and kneepad into his pants. I boiled his mouthpiece and had him bite down and make his teeth impression. I put on his shoulder pads and cleats. It was one of the proudest days of my life as a father. My son, my little man, my seed was about to embark on a journey to become the next great football legend. Or so I thought.

When we got to the football field, I took Marcus out of the seat belt and told him to grab his helmet. As he ran across the field toward the other little boys, my chest was puffed out like a body builder on steroids. He joined in with the other little boys as they began to do warm-up exercises. His helmet was bouncing around on his little head, making him look like a bobblehead. I would see him looking at me for approval after every exercise. A father's affirmation is essential to the growth and development of his child.

A son wants to know that the way he is living his life—his interests, schoolwork, hobbies, and passions—is pleasing to his father. And as a good dad, it is critical for a father to guide his son into right actions and help him live a life centered on serving others (Warren 2013).

Marcus at five years old was attempting to form a bond, a bond with me his father because deep down inside, he wanted my approval. This was done without thought or premeditation. This means that children need, crave, and depend on the approval of their fathers to help them grow into productive people. When children don't receive that affirmation, they spend their whole lives looking for it through women, drugs, gangs, and achievement.

List five goals you have as a father for your children.

1. _____

2. _____

3. _____

4. _____

5. _____

> A child wants to know that the ways they are living their life — their interest, schoolwork, hobbies, and passions — are pleasing to their father. And, as a good dad, it is critical for a father to guide his child into right actions and help them live a life centered on serving others. (Roland C. Warren)

After the exercise portion of practice was over, the kids were placed into a circle, and the coach started pairing the boys off according to size and height. The coach then simply said, "Oklahoma drill." This is when two people are placed in the center of the group circle and made to simulate the snap of the ball and fire off like offensive and defensive linemen. Several of veteran players went first, and you could hear the helmets and pad popping. The coaches were getting excited as the drill became more and more intense.

Finally, it was my son's turn. I had gotten so wrapped up in watching the other little boys perform the drill I had stopped concentrating on what Marcus was doing. When I looked at him, I saw the fear and discomfort in his eyes, but I felt like this could toughen him up. They lined Marcus up, and then the other young man was placed in his stance. The coach gave the boys their instructions. He said, "When I say hike, fire off the ball and try to push each other backwards." At this point, Marcus was crying, and tears were running down his face.

Coach then says "hike," and the other young man does exactly what the coach says—he fires off the ball low and fast. Marcus, however, stands straight up and is blasted backward to the ground. The cry becomes louder now, and Marcus begins to say, "Daddy, I don't want to play," over and over again. I told him to get up and stop acting like a baby. I allowed them to place him back on the line and try again; however, we got the same result. Marcus stood straight up. The other young man fired off the ball low and fast, and Marcus went backward and to the ground. He was in obvious distress, but I lack the knowledge or ability to be a father to my son at that moment in time in his life. This is something that still haunts me to this day. I wish I would have known then what I know now about what it means to be a father.

Instead of me being the protector for my son, I was embarrassed that he was crying, and I yelled at him to stop crying. I still can remember me screaming at my son like he had done something wrong when in actuality it was me who had placed him in an uncomfortable environment, which was not conducive to his success.

Being stubborn, I continued to impose my will on my son. This led to resentment, bitterness, and anger on his part. These issues plagued our relationship for years. I have learned over the years that fathers should try not to upset their children because it can lead to the deterioration of the relationship.

> And, ye fathers provoke not your children to wrath: but nurture them in the chastening and admonition of the Lord. (Eph. 6:4, NKJV)

Many men like me have no true idea of what it means to be a father or what we should be doing to guarantee that our children are successful in the future. We must begin a process of mentoring men so that they can return and mentor their own children. We have reached a day and time where we can no longer assume that men know what to do to become an effective father. There are three key essentials a man must know to understand his purpose in the family: authoritative, visionary, and provider.

First, fathers must be *authoritative*. They should be the first person in the life of their children to show authority. Fathers should teach their children discipline and respect for authority. They should give a regimen that improves disciplinary skills. Fathers should provide his children with knowledge of why it is important to respect others. They should be firm and fair. This helps teach the child the importance of submitting to authority. It is important that children learn this at an early age because in some form or fashion, they will be submitting to authority for the rest of their lives. Whether it is in school, work, or just in social settings, understanding the authority structure is crucial to your success. Ultimately, it is the responsibility of the father to provide guidance and structure in the life of his child. In chapter 6, I will dig deeper into this concept of submission to authority.

> Listen, there is no way any true man is going to let children live around him in his home and not discipline and teach, fight and mold them until they know all he knows. His goal is to make them better than he is. Being their friend is a distant second to this. (Victor Devlin)

Second, a father must be a *visionary*. He should give vision to the family and provide a sense of direction for life.

When I drive around Memphis, I see kids hanging out on the corner at all times of the night, and it makes me wonder where their fathers are. A good father will help his children find purpose for their life. He should teach his children that their life has purpose and meaning and teach them how to develop that purpose and chase after their passion.

When my daughter Mykaela was four years old, she came to me with a sad look on her face and said, "Daddy, what is my thing? Marcus is good at drawing. What am I good at?"

I looked at her, and without hesitation, I told her that she was great at reading and storytelling. I encouraged her to continue reading as many books as she could because one day, she may just become an author. Her face lit up. She was so excited because I had told her she was good at something, and I helped her gain self-confidence about reading. At fifteen years old in the ninth grade, she recently scored a 21 on her ACT and is reading on a grade 12 level. The encouragement I gave on that day has stayed with her ever since and has molded her into an exceptional reader and student.

Fathers should also encourage and motivate their children to chase their dreams and goals and celebrate their accomplishments. Fathers should always teach their children to go after the things that make them happy. Fathers should pour their knowledge into their children to help them understand the importance of pursuing their passion. Encouraging them in the things that they are good at, saying to them that they are great and have been blessed with personalized talents and skills, which are essential to their success.

> My father always told me, Find a job you love and you will never work a day in your life! (Jim Fox)

Lastly, fathers should be *providers* spiritually, financially, and emotionally. Fathers should teach their children the importance of having a spiritual relationship with God. This helps them understand that life is about more than just them. It helps them know that they have someone to lean on when life knocks them down. It also gives them comfort to know that they have a heavenly protector to watch over them daily.

Fathers have to understand that they are financially responsible for food, clothing, and shelter. Whether a father is in the home or not, it is his duty to provide financially for his child's well-being. If you are not working, then you should provide your time as compensation for your lack of financial support. Men often think that money is the most important thing they can give, and that is simply not the case. Quality time is essential to the father-child relationship. Spending time shows that you are available. It shows your child that they are your priority, and most importantly, it shows that you care. At the end of the day, what our kids want to know most is that we care.

Fathers should provide a safe environment for their children to grow. A man's top priority is to protect the innocence of his children at all cost. When our children are exposed to sex, violence, and drugs at an early age, it steals the natural innocence that they were born with. Providing your children with a listening ear also gives them comfort that you have their best interest at heart. Hearing the concerns of your child also helps to build unbreakable bonds that last a lifetime. Provide room for mistakes and growth through transparency. A father should share his fears, failures, and fortunes with his children. This helps your children see that through life's adversity, true character is built. Sharing fears will help children overcome their own fears. Sharing failures shows children you can bounce back from hard times. Sharing fortunes shows children that adversity does not come to stay it comes to pass.

> Fathers are vital to the family dynamic and need to return! (MeiAngelo Taylor)

List three of each of your fears, failures, and fortunes.

Fears

1. _____

2. _____

3. _____

Failures

1. _____
2. _____
3. _____

Fortunes

1. _____
2. _____
3. _____

2

Breaking Family Cycles

> So the story of a man runs in a dreary circle, because he is not yet master of the earth that holds him! (Will Durant)

In order to become the man or father you were designed to be, you must have a clear understanding of your family history. How will you know where you are going if you don't know where you have come from? As far back as I can remember, my life has been filled with, let's just say adversity! *Adversity* is defined by dictionary.com as "adverse fortune or fate; a condition marked by misfortune, calamity, or distress; unfortunate event or circumstances." I would say adversity is the perfect word to describe my life. There have been some good days and bad days, but the common thread to them all has been adversity.

I was born on February 6, 1977, to Delores and Waverly Taylor. My parents loved me, but there were flaws in their relationship. My father was in the military and had begun to show signs of mental instability. My mother was a proud spicy woman who could curse out a stop sign. Together, they were like dynamite. They would argue and fight almost daily. In the late seventies and early eighties, domestic violence was not taken as serious as it is today; and if it was, let's just say both of my parents would have been incarcerated.

Even as a young child, I can remember the tension in the house when my parents would argue and fight. I remember one particular argument that became so heated that my mother received a stab wound to her leg. My father had a pot of boiling hot water thrown at him. My father, in a rage of anger, shot a gun into my grandparents' home because my mother would not talk to him. These are just microcosms of the domestic violence I saw as a child. Domestic violence can have long-term effects on the victim and their children (348).

According to domesticviolencestatistics.org, "Up to 10 million children witness some form of domestic violence annually." I believe that the violence I witnessed as a child played a huge role in my poor childhood development. I was an angry, confrontational child who would act out often that had a lack of conflict resolution skills. My problem solving skills were limited. I had low assessment of verbal, motor, and cognitive skills. Children in families experiencing domestic violence are more likely than other children to exhibit aggressive and antisocial behavior or to be depressed and anxious (Brown and Bzostek 2003).

Most experts believe that children who are raised in abusive homes learn that violence is an effective way to resolve conflicts and problems. They may replicate the violence they witnessed as children in their teen and adult relationships and parenting experiences (domesticviolencerountable.org). Boys who witness their mothers' abuse are more likely to batter their female partner as adults than boys raised in nonviolent homes (Putnam 2004). Domestic violence on any level can be detrimental to the development of children. Parents, listen please. It is your job to protect the innocence of your children for as long as heavenly possible. Once a child's innocence has been stolen, it can never be given back. People must get educated about the lasting devastating affects domestic violence plays on the entire family structure.

The devastating effect it played on my family was that my mother and father separated. And in the early eighties, my mother, brother, and I moved from Memphis to San Francisco. For the first time in our lives, we were away from my grandparents. California seemed a great place for our family. When we moved to San Francisco, we lost most contact with my biological father. My momma began to work as a teacher-assistant at Balboa High School and part-time at the local answering service company on the night shift. Things seemed to be looking up for us. The fighting and arguing had stopped, but what took its place was just as bad, if not worse.

My mother was living in a new city with no family around. She became lonely and a coworker Celestine introduced my mother to her brother, Robert. He had been recently released from jail, and they began to date. Robert was a tall dark skinned man. He stood about 6'2" 175 lbs. and just had this no nonsense demeanor. I was resentful because my mother had a new man who was attempting to assume the role of my father. Meanwhile, I started kindergarten at Fairmont Elementary where I struggled mightily. While I was struggling with school, Renaldo was flourishing. He is three years older than me and always had done well with school.

Once my mother began dating Robert, our lives were never the same. Robert introduced my mother to hardcore drugs (i.e., powder cocaine, heroin, crack cocaine and pills). The drugs had a tremendous effect on all our lives. The drugs took control of her life rapidly. Within months of becoming addicted, she lost both of her jobs. We started having strangers over to the house at all times of the day and night. The one thing I remembered and always thought to be weird was the amount of time spent in the bathroom. If you know anyone who has struggled with addiction, you understand what I mean by that last statement.

Addicts spend an absorbent amount of their time in the bathroom whispering!

To support their habit, my stepfather would resort to crime. He would steal clothes off the back of delivery trucks on Market Street in San Francisco. He would burglarize homes and even committed robberies all in an effort to support their drug habit. They would sometimes even make me and my brother get involved in the act. We would go into Macy's Department Store with oversized clothes on, and they would make us put new clothes underneath our old clothes and walk out the store. This was in the early eighties long before the days of sensors were being placed in the clothes. Addiction turned our family once with an educator and believer as the head into a den of thieves.

Because of his criminal activity, my stepfather would spend lots of time in and out of jail. When he would get locked up, my mother would see other men to help pay for her habit. One man in particular was named Tony. He would come by the house from time to time and even spend the night occasionally. However, after a few months, he stopped coming over; and anytime he would call the house for my mother, she would have either my brother or me say that she was not home. Something had happened, but we were too young to grasp what was going on because she was obviously avoiding contact with Tony. Looking back on it, perhaps it was because my stepfather was about to be released from jail.

Several weeks after my stepfather was released, we (my brother, mother, stepfather, and myself) were all at the neighborhood grocery store, and Tony walked in and saw mother and approached her and said, "Where the "F" is my money, "b?" Robert stepped in front of my mother and began to argue with Tony.

Tony stated, "When y'all get outside, I'm gone beat your ass."

When they got outside, they continued to argue. My brother and I were scared, and I was crying because Tony was a bigger man, and I didn't want him to hurt Robert. Once outside, the two men squared up, and Tony swung at Robert, but he ducked. When he ducked, he slipped and fell. Tony then kicked Robert in the ribs, and Robert fell backward. Just as it seemed like Tony was going to get the best of Robert, Tony slipped because he was wearing snake-skinned boats. When he slipped, Robert punched him in the jaw and jumped on top of him and kept hitting him in the face. Seconds later, Robert went into his pocket and pulled out a pocket knife and stabbed Tony several times in the abdomen, causing him serious injury.

By this time, we could hear police sirens in the background. Right before the police arrived, Robert got up and slid the knife he had to a neighborhood friend. When the police arrived on the scene, they handcuffed Robert. My mother went crazy. She started saying he didn't do anything. She started cursing at the officers on the scene, and she was so belligerent that even though she was not involved in the fight, she was arrested as well for disorderly conduct. In my mother behest to defend my stepfather, she forgot about her sons. What would happen to us if she and Robert were arrested?

When the ambulance arrived, Tony was taken to the hospital in serious condition. Thankfully, he eventually was able to make a full recovery. After this incident, we never heard from him again. Robert was charged with assault. We were told that we would have to stay with mother goose until my Mother was released from jail. While staying with mother goose, we had the privilege of watching her cook up her heroine and shoot up right in front of us as if she was teaching us how to make ice cream for the first time. She took out her needle, spoon, cotton balls, lighter, and a belt to tie off. I was four years old, and to this day, I still remember her talking to us while she was preparing her drugs. She said, "Y'all don't ever need to try this stuff. It can kill you!" When she stuck that needle into her arm, she slowly lay back on the couch; and her eyes rolled back in her head, and she started rubbing her arms until she was completely silent and still. I was terrified and just tried to focus on the TV that was in the room. We stayed in her home for two days, but it seemed like a lifetime. My parents' struggle with addiction and mental illness had a profound impact on my life.

> Those who don't know their history are doomed to repeat it! (Edmund Burke)

Because of the struggles my parents faced, I had a difficult childhood. I was an angry child and had problems adapting at school. In kindergarten, I took a knife to school because I planned to stab a fifth grade boy who had been bullying me. I cursed out my teacher and called her a "bald head "b." I refused to do work because I struggled with reading. I remember getting whooped because I struggled with reading and spelling. I would constantly stay in the office due to disciplinary issues.

I struggled with self-esteem issues as a result of being abandoned by my parents. In my teen years, I continued to struggle in school, not because I was dump, but because I found it kind of difficult to focus on my studies when I didn't know if the lights would be on when I got home from school. When you don't know where your parents are, your priorities have a tendency to change. There would be days at a time that I had no clue where my mother was, and my father was halfway across the country dealing with his own issues. Either way, they were not there to take care of me. I felt alone, heartbroken, disappointed, and scared many nights.

In my adult years, I struggled in my relationships because I never dealt with the issues of abandonment from my childhood. I never felt that anyone ever loved me. I thought that the women in my life would always leave me just as my mother and father had done as a child. Therefore, I built up a wall to guard my feeling so that I wouldn't be abandoned ever again. In order to move forward in life, we must successfully overcome past hurts and disappointments. Your family history can affect your life now and in the future!

Who hurt you or disappointed you? was the question I had to ask myself. What has happened in your life to hold back your growth? Are you willing to discuss it let it go? I had to address the fact that my parents were not there for me the way that I needed them to be. I had to acknowledge that my mother chose drugs over us, her children. I had to accept that we can never go back and change our past; we can only learn from it and try to do better in our future. I had to believe that I could get pass the hurt and disappointment.

Once I realized that there is power in the ability to discuss my issues and that I could be free from burden, it changed my life. There was no need to be embarrassed to say that my father struggled with mental illness, that my mother was addicted to drugs, that as a young man I was angry and aggressive. I am free from the bondage of my past because I have embraced it and known that all my struggles were simply a part of the plan to get me to where God desires me to be. Now, I have an understanding of the how my family history affects my ability to be a good man, husband, and father. I first had to have a desire to understand why I was the way I was.

Most men, oftentimes, are not willing to evaluate their families and uncover the secrets that help tell the stories of who they are or could possibly become. We allow ourselves to be blindfolded by the things in life that don't really matter, like how many women you have, what type of car you drive, or how much money you make. All of which are like illusions; they are not real or tangible things that can help save our eternal soul. Oftentimes, we men allow distraction to keep us from purpose and destiny!

> When the soul of a man is born in this country there are nets flown at it to hold it back! (James Joyce)

Activity

Identify and write down one past hurt or disappointment faced in your childhood.

_____

_____

_____

There's nothing like an understanding. When we begin to understand what holds us back, we can then begin the process to conquer that which hinders our growth. We become powerful when we gain knowledge of our self-destructive behaviors. These behaviors can lead to terrible decisions, which can cause life-altering outcomes. Usually, these decisions are made impulsively without thought. As a result of impulsive decisions, I have a strained relationship with a daughter whom I rarely see.

Identification is the first step to overcoming the issues in your life. Not identifying my issues with abandonment affected every relationship I had. The abandonment left me with an in ability to trust women. Therefore, it became easy to be a manipulator, to be verbally and physically abusive, and to sleep with as many women as I possibly could without remorse or guilt.

Activity

Identify and write down one thing you can do to recognize when you are allowing this issue to overtake your thoughts and emotions.

_____

_____

_____

Before anyone can become a manipulator, they must form some level of rationale that will allow them to justify their actions. I had formulated in my mind that if my mother and father had left me, so would any woman; after al,l they were supposed to be there for me through thick and thin. So when I treated women bad or cheated on, I felt justified in my actions because my mind was toxic.

The biggest self-destructive behavior that I struggled with was sex. I used sex as a tool of revenge. I used sex to help me deal with being rejected in my relationships. If I was ever denied sexual relations, I felt it was right to go and get involved in illicit sexual activity with other women. Again, I don't condone it. I'm just sharing where my head was at during that time in my life.

Because I opened myself up to these behaviors, they are something that I will have to deal with for the rest of my life. I became addicted to sexual lust, and like any addict, there are steps I will have to take for the rest of my life not to fall back into that type of sexual perversion. However, now that I know what my demons are, I am better able to fight back when I am attacked in the area of sexual immorality.

Activity

Identify and write down one to three destructive self-behaviors that have affected your life.

1. _____

2. _____

3. _____

I have discussed how our family history can affect our present, past, and future circumstances. I have shown why it is important to face these issues head-on in an attempt to move forward and grow as human beings. I looked at how identifying, acknowledging, and accepting responsibility for self-destructive behaviors can bring about growth in my life.

3

Check Yourself

> You are the only common denominator in everything that has happened to you in life, be it good or bad. To learn / grow from these experiences, you must accept the role you played in each of them!
> (AC Anderson)

"Enough is enough! Momma, why? Why are you doing this again? The drugs are killing you, Momma! Tell me who gave you those drugs! Don't lie to me, Momma. I love you! You know what, I know who gave them to you, and tonight, I'm gone do something about it! Get away from me, Momma!" As I run to the front of the house, I had sadness in my heart and murder on my mind. For years, I had watched my mother struggle with addiction. Addiction led my mother to prostitution and us being homeless. I even saw my mother beaten with a bat over drugs. I had grown tired of watching her struggle with this addiction. I was tired of being disappointed and hurt.

I drove to a friend's house and said, "Man, let me borrow your gun." Come to think of it, he never even asked what I needed it for. He just said, "Sure." When I got that gun, I had every intention of killing the man who had given my mother that crack cocaine. I drove to Michael's house, and when I got out the car, I took that gun and placed it in the small of my back and walked up to the door.

When I got to the door, I was scared but determined to end Michael's life. I knocked on the door. *Boom! Boom!* No one answered, so I knocked again. *Boom! Boom! Boom!* Finally, Michael came to the door, and before he had a chance to say a word, I pulled that gun from behind my back, and I pointed the gun in his face. "Tell me, did you sell my mother those drugs? And if you lie, I am going to blow your brains all over this floor." As I pointed the gun at him, I noticed that my hand was shaking!

Just as Michael was about to speak, his two-year-old niece, Mariah, walked to the door. I looked down at her and quickly placed the gun behind my back, started crying, and ran back to the car. I like to think that Mariah was my guardian angel that night because if she hadn't come to the door, I know that I would have shot Michael and most likely ended up in jail.

When I got back to the car, I can remember driving and crying out to God, saying, "God, why is my family this way? Why must we go through so many trials and tribulations?" I started to wonder if she would ever stop, or if our lives would ever get better? And in my moment of sadness and depression, I had a thought. Maybe if I kill myself, maybe she will see how bad she was hurting her children. I almost gave up on life and missed my opportunity to help others. What I have found is that sometimes in our most difficult moments in life, we can find our greatest purpose!

I took that gun and placed it to my head. I was so exhausted with the hand that I had been dealt in life. Tired of always ending up with the short end of the stick so to speak. So I did place the gun to my head, and just as I was about to pull the trigger, I heard a voice. The voice of God said to me, *It is not your time. I have more for you to do!* I threw the gun down in the seat and continued to drive and cry out to God. I said, "I don't ever want my children to live the way I'm living. I don't want them to see the things I have seen!" In my mind, I felt perhaps my death would bring about some sort of guilt that would convince her to change her life and stop using drugs.

I wanted to hurt her the same way she had been hurting us. For years, she had put the drugs before us, and it hurt. We felt that we were not important to her. I felt as if my life was void of meaning and or purpose. I couldn't believe it at the time that I had something to give society. What

I now know about addiction is that my death would not have made a difference; she more than likely would have sunk deeper into addiction because of the guilt she possibly would have felt. The only thing that stops addiction is the person having the desire and discipline to make the change in their own life. Her addiction would not let her see or understand the pain her actions were causing.

Enough Is Enough Activity

Write down the issues in your life that you are tired of struggling with.

_____

_____

_____

Looking back over my life, that was a pivotal moment. It was the first time in my life that I started to believe that maybe there was a plan for my life. Maybe, just maybe God had heard my cries. For years, I had listened to my elder's say that if you have a problem, just pray about it, and God will hear you and answer your prayers. I was sixteen years old when I walked into that room and saw my mother using crack cocaine, just sixteen, and I thought I was a man. That night, my emotions were all over the place. I went from committing suicide to looking into my future, wanting to be a better man and father for my own children. I became so fed up that I confronted my past and decided that my life would be different.

Confronting your past is the only way to move forward in life. In order for men to be freed of their past, they must first be willing to confront the things that haunt and hurt them. Men must learn how to forgive people who have hurt them so that they can have a clear conscience. Forgiving others oftentimes has nothing to with that person but much to do with us letting go of the past. Forgiveness is for you so that you can keep going and keep growing! You cannot be an effective leader for your children or family if you have not addressed the issues of your own past!

> It is necessary for a man to go away by himself ... to go away by himself ... to sit on a rock ... and ask, "Who am I, where have I been, and where am I going?" (Carl Sandburg)

Activity

Promise to confront those issues today! List your action steps!

_____

_____

Oftentimes, men must face insurmountable odds and struggles in order to find the strength to fight for our lives. The question then becomes, how do we confront our past? Once you realize that you need to make changes, what should you do? Should you be ashamed of the things in your past? Can you overcome you past and succeed?

Three Steps to Confronting Your Past

First, men must not be afraid to look into their future. Looking into your future gives you hope that things can get better. Men must start seeing themselves as they hope to be, instead of where they are now. The night I almost shot Michael and almost committed suicide, I didn't realize it. But then but when I said, "I don't ever want my children to grow up the way I had grown up," I took a journey into my future, and it gave me the hope I needed to continue going on with life. They became my why.

You must have a why, a reason that during tough times can motivate you to keep going and not give up. Life will throw you a few curve balls, and having a why can help you keep focused on the task at hand. Having a why also makes life about others and not just yourself. For me, my why was to let my friends and family know that their struggles were not in vain. I want to let my parents know that because of their struggles, I have gained a compassion for the sufferings of the human race. Now more than ever,

I appreciate the difficulties I faced as a child because it has molded me into the man I am today.

I have had many people who were close to me passing away either from illness or homicide. In 1989, my stepfather (Robert) passed away due to complication from HIV. In 2001, one of my best friends was shot in the head at a nightclub, and I had to tell his mother that he had been murdered. In 1999, my grandfather died from complications with diabetes. He was the rock of our family. My father continues his struggle with mental illness. My mother has been clean and sober for seven years now. These and many others including my wife and children are my whys.

I have decided to tell our stories. Even though some of my friends and family are dead and gone, their lives will go on through me! I have made a covenant promise to share their stories with the world and use the pain in their lives to encourage, help, and motivate others. Now as I go chase my passion to see men reconnected to their children, I don't go at it alone. I have an army of people whose backs I am standing on. During tough times, I think about them I how much I owe them for the life I have today, and I become so grateful. What is your reason for being? Hold onto it during difficult and depressing times!

What Does the Future Hold?

1. What's your why, the reason to keep you going when times get hard?

   _____

   _____

   _____

Second, men must stop running away from adversity. I told you earlier in this book that when I found out I had gotten Gloria pregnant, I ran. I ran because I was scared, scared of all the responsibility that comes along with being a father. However, what I know now is that adversity is designed to make you stronger. I'm so glad that Gloria did not allow me to be that coward, and that she challenged me to be a father. I am so thankful to have a relationship with all my children. I also know that I have made many mistakes in my life in regards to my children, but I believe they all know deep down inside that I love them dearly and would do anything to see them become successful in life.

If I would have continued to run away from my responsibility, I would not have known the joy of watching my children grow up and exceed all my wildest expectations. How will you ever know what you are made of if you never face your adversity? Men tend to see adversity as something meant to hold them back. I, however, now see adversity as something designed to make me stronger, for the plans that God has for my life. I embrace it now because I have matured and realize that diamonds are made under pressure!

What Haven't You Faced?

1. What adversity is holding you back from meeting your potential?

   _____

   _____

Lastly, it is vitally important for men to realize that change is a process. Change takes time. Are you willing to take the time to go through your process? Most people cannot endure the process, so they give up or quit before any significant change can ever take place. They then complain about where they are in life.

There is a story about two men in separate tunnels digging for gold. Both men have the same pick axe. Both men are faithful; they get up early in the morning and go to their dig site and begin digging. However, several months into the dig, one man starts to become discouraged and starts to believe that perhaps he has picked the wrong site to dig at while the other man stays faithful to the process and just continues to believe that he is in the right place at the right time, and at some point, he will strike gold. Just as the man became doubtful and gave up, the man who believed continued to dig and struck the wall one more time, and that's when he struck gold. The moral behind that story is, no matter how unrealistic a situation may look, if we keep believing and keep picking away at it, something has to give.

With God's grace and mercy, have the ability to overcome any obstacle we may face in life, if we understand that change is a process that happens over time. The wonderful thing that I have realized about change is that the moment you desire change in your life, you have already begun the process to see that change take place. In order for anything to come into being, it must first start as a thought. From thought, it must become an action; and from action, it can become your reality!

I am more than my scars! (Andrew Davidson)

Are you willing to go through your process of change?

1. Understanding that change is a process, are you willing to keep going and keep growing? What will be your first steps of change?

   _____

   _____

4

Man Up!

> Man needs his difficulties because they are necessary to enjoy success.
>
> —A. P. J. Abdul Kalam

A Ben & Jerry's moment. A day of complete and total honesty. This was the day I took my oldest daughter, Imani, to eat ice cream; and more importantly, it gave her a chance to talk to me about her feelings toward me. I talked to her about my mistakes as her father. I admitted that it bothered me that we didn't live in the same city, and I knew that I had done more with my other children than I did with her. I talked about me not knowing the right way to be her father in the early years. I took responsibility for our troubled relationship.

According to examiner.com (2010),

> Children and adults alike should *always* be held accountable for their choices, actions, and/or behaviors no matter how big or how small. Adults have an obligation and higher duty to their children to teach them that functioning within a society means abiding by boundaries and limitations and more importantly respecting the boundaries of others.
>
> Parents need to teach their children how to solve their problems through appropriate measures so they can interact on a responsible social and personal level. One of the best ways in which to do this is through role modeling. So not only do adults need to be responsible for the actions, they need to consistently step up while still standing by their child and enforce accountability.

It was a setting in which both of us had a chance to share our feelings openly and honestly. The conversation was without any outside interference. I was not talking to her through her mother nor was she talking to me through her mother. I was willing to answer any questions that she had for me without hesitation. I had already decided to be as transparent as I could possibly be.

When the gloves come off, men must be prepared for whatever is said. If she had told me that she hated me and never wanted anything to do with me, I had to be prepared to work through that hurt with her. I understand that when children have anger toward their fathers, it is normally because they have been hurt and disappointed. When hurt, your children will initially resist you. However, anything worth having is worth working for, and there is no greater relationship than that of the father and his children.

Children are like onions. You must be willing to peel back the layers of disappointment. This is done over time through love and patience. It is important for men who have not been on the lives of their children to understand that they cannot immediately step back in and just assume the role of disciplinarian in the lives of their children. This will lead to more and more resistance from your child and can lead to a permanent strain on the relationship. The ultimate goal of the father should be to build a lasting relationship that develops love, respect, and trust. Trust is the key to making it happen; it is the only way to break down the walls that have been built in the relationship. Here's an article from drphil.com:

> "The time for blaming, regretting and apologizing is over," says Dr. Frank Lawlis in his book, Mending the Broken Bond. If you are ready to be the parent your child needs you to be, follow the four steps below to put the past behind you, change your approach to parenting that has not worked, and focus on what lies ahead.
>
> 1. Step Up and Be the Role Model Your Child Needs
>
> Your job as a role model begins when your child is born — there is no avoiding that responsibility.

It is important that you live up to your end of the parental contract. "You've got to stand up and give it your best at all times," Dr. Lawlis says. "Most parents don't realize that they are the most important figures in their children's lives from day one."

Your child has been studying you and been picking up on our moods since he/she was 1 month old. "As children grow older, they learn to judge what their parents' responses will be based on moods, facial expressions, tone of voice and other subtle clues."

You are your child's guide to the world. It's OK if you're not perfect, but be your best. It's important that your child sees your effort.

2. Walk Your Talk

"If you don't stand for something, you will fall for anything," says Dr. Lawlis. "The effort and courage you put into following these values communicates their importance to your children." It is important that you set out values, principles and guidelines for your child and make sure he/she understands that you expect him/her to follow them. Children get in trouble when they don't have guidelines. "Until they are mature adults, they need guidance, and they will follow your example, whether good or bad."

Strive to live up to the guidelines you set for your family. If you fail to do so, your children will call you on it and ask for an explanation.

3. Open the Lines of Communication

"Believe it or not, children secretly want to put down the video game controllers and talk to you," Dr. Lawlis reveals. "They want to share their lives with you, and they want to know what is on your mind, but they are waiting for signs that you are listening." When your children speak to you, listen closely, but also watch what they are telling you through emotions, gestures and level of excitement. It is important to build a strong foundation of mutual trust and understanding while your child is young, so it is in place as he/she grows older.

4. Always Find a Common Ground

"It is also vital that you establish a negotiating forum that allows both sides to walk away winners," Dr. Lawlis says. When you finish a conversation with your child, you should both feel the benefits. Play a game with your child where everyone rejoices when someone wins. "It's not about who wins or loses. It is the shared enthusiasm in support of each other."

Find out what their interests and hobbies are and make a connection through those outlets. If your child likes sports, go watch their favorite team with them! If they are into trains, take them to watch trains leaving the station. Whatever it is, just get involved in their lives the fastest way to get yourself reconnected to them. It is not just about the money that is spent; it is more about the time that you have invested into the relationship.

In rebuilding the trust, attempt to do whatever you say you will do. It is very important to stay consistent when rebuilding a relationship. It helps your children reestablish faith in you. Also know that it is okay to say, "I can't do it right now." Kids don't expect Superman! We often think our children are looking for perfection, and oftentimes, they are not. They desire consistent relationship with us as fathers. If you stay consistent, you will be well on your way to rebuilding the relationship.

When building on a future, it will be important to start making new memories for the future. One of the things I did was to not let the past keep me from making new more desirable memories. The best way to remove bad memories is to create new good ones. Start spending time with your children, take them to a movie, or go to their favorite restaurant.

If you make your children a priority in your life, they will appreciate it and grow to respect you for it. By putting the needs of your children before your own, you show them how to live a life of service. Teaching them that true happiness comes when we all place the needs of others before our own. If done properly, your children will develop a selfless attitude toward community, helping and serving others.

It is important to communicate your circumstances with your kids. They need to know what is going on in your life. Kids respect your honesty. Your relationship will grow from these moments of honesty you share with them. Your ability to communicate openly with your children is how you win their trust back in the long run. Ask your children for forgiveness; it shows them that you acknowledge the wrong done to them by you.

When I talked to my oldest daughter about the mistakes I had made, she just listened attentively. She forgave me, a man who ran from his responsibility. A man whom she would see only during the summer, thought he had the right to discipline her without ever really knowing her. A man who had not been there for her the way I should have. A man who abandoned her and had other children after her that I had a closer relationship with.

Perhaps she saw the humility in my eyes when we talked. Maybe she heard the sincerity in my voice as I shared with her how I made decision after decision that put my own selfish wants and needs before hers. She could have seen the tears in my eyes as I told her that I loved her and wanted to start our relationship over, and that I would work harder to be a better man and father going forward.

According to artofmanliness.com (2009),

> The definition of humility need not include timidity or becoming a wallflower. Instead, humility simply requires a man to think of his abilities and his actions as no greater, and no lesser, than they really are. Real humility then mandates that a man knows

and is completely honest with himself. He honestly assesses what are, and to what magnitude he possess talents and gifts, struggles and weaknesses.

Humility is the absence of pride. We are taught to think pride is a good thing. But pride functions only when comparing others to yourself. Don't base your self-worth on how you stack up to others. Instead, focus on yourself and how you can improve.

According to scotthyoung.com (2008),

> Beyond personal success, humility is also a virtue for inner well-being. Frustrations and losses don't have the same impact if you don't get your ego involved. If you combine humility with motivation, you have the ability to drive toward successes without letting the failures knock you out of balance.

Interesting Fact

Youth in father-absent households still had significantly higher odds of incarceration than those in mother-father families (Harper and McLanahan 2004).

To share your weakness is to make yourself vulnerable; to make yourself vulnerable is to show your strength! (Criss Jami)

Transparency Game

Take two to three minutes and practice in the mirror or with someone you trust and open up, verbally saying what it is that he has done wrong and what you can do better in the relationship.

The purpose of this is to prepare the men to be able to verbalize their feeling in an environment of support, toleration, and love! This will help men be better equipped to communicate with their children. When you gain the ability to be open, honest, and forthcoming, your words become more powerful, and people will listen!

5

Fatherless Landfills

> Kids have a hole in their soul in the shape of their dad. And if a father is unwilling or unable to fill that hole, it can leave a wound that is not easily healed.
> (Roland Warren)

A Flawed System

"A system of trash and garbage disposal in which the waste is buried between layers of earth to build up low-lying land." According *Merriam-Webster*, this is the definition of a *landfill*. It also closely resembles what we as men have allowed to happen in the lives of our children. We have allowed our most precious commodity to be thrown in the landfill of life. Children all across this nation and the world are being disposed of in the low-lying sanitary landfills. However, we as men are not alone in the blame for this problem! There are three key components. Two of which I will address in this chapter: child support system and women.

The most important word in the definition of landfill is system. According to *Merriam-Webster*, a *system* is an "organized set of doctrines, ideas, or principles usually intended to explain the arrangement or working of a systematic whole." In this particular case, the juvenile court system has played a large role in fathers being absent from the lives of their children. I have talked to hundreds of men over the years, and almost all of them have a distrust of the juvenile court system. They have a lack of trust for and fell as if they have been mistreated by the court system.

Time and time again, the men I have spoken with have said when dealing with juvenile court, they did not believe that they would be given a fair chance. Many of them feel as though they are being slighted by the system. They become bitter and angry and feel their only recourse is not to have any interaction with the children as a form of punishment, which only hurts the development of the child.

The Elephant in the Room

1. Trust among men for the juvenile court system almost _____.

2. Men are _____ and _____ because they feel Juvenile Court is a one-sided system!

In my humbled opinion, the child support system should be revamped. I completely understand the importance of financial support, but it fails in comparison to emotional and relational support. If we see that a system we have in place is broken, why is it so hard to admit it is flawed and make the necessary changes to move forward. The definition of insanity is doing the same thing over and over and expecting different results. Our children are growing up without discipline and guidance simply because a man does not have the financial means to support them. American children are becoming more and more defiant toward authority, because there is no true authority structure in the family anymore.

With the evolution of social media, our children are seeing and hearing more immorality than at any other time in the history of the world. Fathers are needed now more than ever. Daughters and sons need the affirmation of their fathers so that they don't spend their lives looking for it in all the wrong places. Our girls are being used for sex and our sons joining gangs, getting involved with drugs. A man with or without financial stability can help with these social ills that we face in society.

The time has come to have legitimate talks about reforming our juvenile court system when it comes to child support. Most importantly, if we change the child support system, it can lead to more positive interaction between parents, which in return is good for the children. According to articles.chicagotribune.com,

> A change in the system aims to curb bitter disputes that tie up courts and can damage a child's relationship with both parents.
>
> "Parents, both mothers and fathers, have talked a lot about making the establishment of child support a more transparent process," says Pam Lowry, head of the state's Division of Child Support Services. "That's exactly what the income shares model does. It's very fair."

The first thing that we need to look at is how we determine monetary support. I think that men who play an active role in the lives of their children should be given credit that applies to their monthly child support. This gives rewards to those who are doing the right thing and gives incentives to those who are not, for them to start doing the right thing. Also for those who are thousands of dollars behind in support, they should be given an opportunity to do community service projects in order to get the amount reduced. For example, cleaning up blighted neighborhoods and cutting grass, becoming after and before school campus monitors. They should be made to attend parenting class, which can also have support fees reduced.

According to articles.chicagotribune.com,

> If a noncustodial parent spends significant time with a child, that likely will be taken into account in calculating the child support obligation. Again, that reflects the modern reality. Kids often spend

huge chunks of time with the noncustodial parent. Why shouldn't that be reflected in the overall child support arrangement?

We must be willing to take drastic measures to see the change in the father child relation in America. Now I know many proponents will say that men should not receive rewards for doing what they should naturally do. In many cases, I would agree; but in this case, I understand the vital role men play in the lives of their children. And I believe that we should do whatever it takes to get men more involved. In states like Ohio, legislators are looking into ways to reform the child support system so that it takes a fair and balance approach providing support.

According to dispatch.com,

> Parents who pay at least half of their court-ordered child support will no longer face suspension of their driver's or professional licenses. The new law — tucked into the recently passed state budget — takes effect on Wednesday. Another provision will allow parents to have prior suspensions for failing to pay child support removed from their driving record. The changes come on the heels of a sentencing-reform law that encourages judges to sentence non-payers to probation or community service instead of jail. The less punitive measures aim to encourage work and seem to buck long-standing practices of cracking down on parents who fail to pay child

support. "The problem is not going to be solved by putting parents in prison or taking away their ability to pay child support," said Donald Hubin, chairman of Fathers and Families of Ohio.

Women's Role

The right of entitlement is when one person or group of persons believes they have more right, importance, or privileges than someone else. Another cog in the wheel of the juvenile court system is mothers. The Juvenile Justice System has either intentionally or unintentionally gave women the confidence to believe that they are the supreme parent, and that they have the final say in what happens with the children.

Among absentee fathers, this is a topic of choice as well. Men often say to me that their children's mothers are denying them access to their children for many reasons that are not valid. I have heard men say that because they have a new girlfriend, she won't let them see their children. Then the women use excuses to justify keeping the father away. Things like you can get your child but you can't take him around your new girlfriend when in all actuality, they don't have the right to make that call. Here is a secret, men. As long as you are not putting your child in any danger, your child's mother can't decide who you bring around your child.

Oftentimes, women use the bitterness of the troubled relationship as a bargaining tool to keep control of the father-child relationship. I have heard women tell men that it doesn't matter what they do; the court system will back them up because they are the mother. I have watched mothers be vindictive toward men who are honestly trying to be there for their children. Men who show up on time try to be role models and still receive pushback.

Entitlement

1. Women feel that they are _____ to certain privileges when it comes to parenting!

2. Mothers often feel they have the right to _____ father's access to their child.

3. Women try to _____ who the father brings around his child.

Let me say this before I am attacked by people thinking that I am bashing women. I think that mothers are doing the best they know how, and that it is the responsibility of men to step up their efforts to become better fathers. I respect, realize, and acknowledge that mothers have been the backbone of the family for many years, and I love them for it. However, I think that there has been a systematic attack on the family structure in America, and I believe that women have been used against men to destroy the family.

In many cases, as a result of the constant pushback, many men have decided to walk away from their children. They simply don't understand that their children are worth the fight. So they walk away and start new lives with new women who are less argumentative and disagreeable. In talking to children, they always ask me how can their father start a new family with new kids and treat them better than they were treated. The answer that I have gotten is that men treat these children differently because the mothers of these children treat them with respect. I would caution women who are struggling with their children's fathers to try a different method to get his attention. Use patience and kindness, and you should see positive change.

> A soft answer turns away wrath: but grievous words stir up anger. (Prov. 15:1, NKJV)

Often, when I talk to single mothers about their child's father, there is a lack of trust and respect. Mothers have grown tired of the excuses. They have been forced to take on the role of both mother and father, because men have not shown a desire to step up and lead their families. As a result, more and more women today believe they don't need a man, which in a sense is also helping to cripple the family structure in America.

According to a blog at yourtango.com,

Danielle Norman stated What really irks me is when I hear women say this in the context of having kids. "I don't need a man to have a baby." It takes both a man and a woman to create one. So actually, you do need a man to have a baby. You may not need to be in a relationship to have a baby, and you may not need a man to help you provide for and raise your child, but you still need one at some point to make the little monster. Even if you use artificial insemination and never meet the father, you still needed him to provide the sperm.

But aside from getting knocked up, do you really need a man? Well, maybe not, but I still find the saying irritating. If you are a lesbian, fine, that makes sense, but I have never heard a lesbian say she doesn't need a man. I have always heard heterosexual women say it and we all know they are full of shit. And the saying is true, but it is only partially so. You may not need a man, but you want one a lot.

I have a friend who I once heard say she didn't need a man. This friend, at the time was so desperately trying to find one though. She wanted to have a good man to love her, and in the way she pursued it, you would think she truly did need a man. If she truly believed that she didn't need a man to be happy, she wouldn't have been trying to find one so badly.

The other day, I heard the results of a study. They had asked a bunch of women and a very large percent of them (somewhere between 60 and 80%)

claimed they could truly be happy without finding love. These were straight women, by the way. And obviously, they were all lying.

I know I have said that I will live if I never find love, but that is very different than saying I'd be truly happy. Maybe some of these women could be, but certainly not as many as claimed to be. Could you be content? Yes. Would it be the end of your life? No. But to be truly happy without love, I think is very difficult to pull off and I think these women are being incredibly disingenuous.

I don't mean to take anything away from the women's movement and all. I just want to point out that there is an epidemic of women thinking they are so much better than men. And that is so wrong. I know that there are bad men in the world, but guess what, there are bad women too. Men have a place on this earth too. And it's not just making babies and moving furniture.

6

Submission to Authority

> True strength lies in the submission which permits one to dedicate his life, through devotion, to something beyond himself. (Henry Miller)

According to mayoclinic.org,

> Oppositional defiant disorder is a pattern of disobedient, hostile, and defiant behavior toward authority figures. Signs of ODD generally begin before a child is eight years old. Sometimes ODD may develop later, but almost always before the early teen years. When ODD behavior develops, the signs tend to begin gradually and then worsen over months or years.

Your child may be displaying signs of ODD instead of normal moodiness if the behaviors:

- Are persistent
- Have lasted at least six months
- Are clearly disruptive to the family and home or school environment

The Following are behaviors associated with ODD:

- Negativity
- Defiance
- Disobedience
- Hostility directed toward authority figures

These behaviors might cause your child to regularly and consistently:

- Have temper tantrums
- Be argumentative with adults
- Refuse to comply with adults request or rules
- Annoy other people deliberately
- Blames others for mistakes or misbehavior
- Act touchy and is easily annoyed
- Feels anger and resentment
- Be spiteful and vindictive
- Act aggressively toward peers

- Have difficulty maintaining friendships
- Have academic problems
- Feels a lack of self esteem

In addition, your child isn't likely to see his or her behavior as defiant. Instead, your child will probably believe that unreasonable demands are being placed on him or her.

Biological Factors

Children and adolescence are more susceptible to developing ODD if they have:

- A parent with a history of attention- deficit/hyperactivity disorder (ADHD), ODD, or CD
- A parent with a mood disorder (such as depression or bipolar disorder)
- A parent who has a problem with drinking or substance abuse
- Impairment in the part of the brain responsible for reasoning, judgement and impulse control
- A brain-chemical imbalance
- A mother who smoked during pregnancy
- Exposure to toxins
- Poor nutrition

Psychological Factors
- A poor relationship with one or more parents
- A negative or absent parent
- A difficulty or inability to form social relationships or process social cues

Social Factors
- Poverty
- Chaotic environment
- Abuse
- Neglect
- Lack of supervision
- Uninvolved parents
- Inconsistent discipline
- Family instability (such as divorce or frequent moves)

What is *authority*? It is the power or right to give orders, make decisions, and enforce obedience. There is a raging debate in America today in regards to how law enforcement in particular white police officers interact with African American males. In recent month, there have been several shootings were unarmed African American young men were gunned down by white police officers, and no punishment was issued in the deaths. As a result, there has been both violent and nonviolent protests all across the country. I want to share with fathers ways they can help to prevent these confrontations that are leading to the deaths of African American boys.

As the decisions were announced in Ferguson, Missouri, and New York, New York, I started to think about ways that I could help to prevent this from happening in the future. One thing that stuck out to me like a sore thumb was, our children needed to learn how to be submissive to authority. More and more children are being raised in single-parent households, without male authority figures. Many of these children will challenge the authority of the people they come in contact with, i.e. teachers, neighbors, and police, and they feel they have the right to be rebellious. They are rebellious toward anyone who attempts to give them corrective instruction. For the past seven years, I've served as a school resource officer within the school system, and I've watched young African American boys become more defiant toward those in authority. I have seen students assault school personnel and have a nonchalant attitude about their behavior.

Rebellion comes from the root word *rebel*, which simply means, "open resistance to," "the refusal to obey," and "to resist authority" (235). There is always a price to pay for rebellious actions (236). When you rebel against authority, you have chosen your course (236). Your rebellion is a magnet for unpleasant things (238). If you want your children to have respect for authority, you must first have respect for authority (238).

Fathers should take responsibility for this lack of respect for authority because it is a father's responsibility to be the first teacher of discipline. Fathers should be the first person to teach his child that we don't always like rules and authority; however, we must obey and respect it. Because fathers have not been there to teach their sons how to interact with authority figures, young men are getting instructions from all the wrong places. Parents must take a stand and not allow our children to make certain decisions for themselves. We must get and stay involved in every aspect of their children's lives (20).

As the father of two African American sons, one of my biggest concerns is how they will interact with law enforcement in the community. I know that not all police see my children as a threat, but in selected cases, many will only see the color of their skin. I try my best to mentally prepare my sons for their inevitable contact with police. I tell them to remember to follow all the rules of the road and always carry themselves in a manner that projects respect.

I consistently try to throw out different scenarios to keep them thinking of ways to get out of compromising positions. I have taught them that when they are in the presence of police personnel, they should say things like, "Yes, sir, or yes, ma'am." I talked to them about understanding that they should try to make their encounter with police as brief as possible. This is done by cooperating and complying with all the officer's commands. Unfortunate as it may be,

I also tell them the reality that sometimes, the police will discriminate against simply them because of the color of their skin.

> **Interesting Fact!**
>
> Oppositional Defiance Disorder affects the lives of girls as well. According to the US Department of Justice (1990), "between 1965 and 1987, the frequency of aggressive acts committed by minors in the United States increased steadily for both sexes. However, the rate for girls increased at a faster rate than that of boys, narrowing the male-female ratio from 11:1 in 1965 to 8:1 in 1987" (Crick 1997, 610).

Aggression among girls is becoming more and more prevalent. The absence of a father from the family structure is causing massive damage to the self-image of girls. As a result, girls are more willing to confront persons in authority and in many cases, be out right defiant. Girls are more aggressive, more likely to fight, and quicker to use a weapon than in past generations.

Girls have become increasingly bitter toward receiving correction. They walk around with more of a chip on their shoulders. They are less likely to forgive a person who has hurt their feelings. Girls have become more apt to seek revenge when they perceive they have been done wrong.

My biggest concern for my daughters is that they get involved in a "female feud." A female feud is when two or more girls who at some point use to be friends, fall out over some trivial thing. It could be because of gossip, jealousy, or over a boy. These feuds lead to constant bickering, arguing, and constant confusion. In the majority of these cases, there is no father or authority figure in place to bring about a positive resolution to the feud or disagreement.

> Girls are more focused on social or relational types of aggression to manipulate and attempt to control others (Crick and Grotpeter 1995). Instead of punches and kicks, girls often use social ostracism, rumor spreading, character assassination, telling falsehoods to manipulate public or individual opinion, and/ or threats to do these things (Crick 1997, SooHoo 2009). Described as "psychological warfare," girl-to-girl bullying (a typical example of social/ relational aggression) is "dehumanizing" and is used … to determine who is valued and who is not … [contributing] to a social hierarchy of privilege and oppression" (SooHoo 2009, 1).
>
> A fool despises his father's instruction. But he who receives correction is prudent! (Prov. 15:5, NKJV)

The music and entertainment industry has become the father figure to today's youth. The music that is promoted to teens today can potentially transform the way they think as a society, all because the system has been bought out and the hidden owners have the agenda that the masses cannot see (21). Today's music teaches people to have little or no respect for authority. These studio gangsters are advising young black men to say, "F the police," which is their first amendment right. However, they are saying these things from the confines of their studios. They have attorneys and record labels backing them, and they have the support to fight charges and incarceration. Most African American young men don't have the resources or the wherewithal to do the same.

Young people are not aware of the plot for their lives. It's similar to a toddler being enticed away by a stranger with candy. Also it is not correct to assume that "clean" music is automatically heavenly. The enemy is very deceitful. A vice-minded composer can also write what appears to be clean music and use it as bait to draw us into evil (4).

Social media has also replaced fathers as role models. Young men look to Facebook, Instagram, Twitter, and other social media sites as guides on to how to live, socialize, and interact with society! Watching videos of people fighting, women twerking, and babies cursing is now all at your fingertips! Quick access to all the things they could ever want without fathers to keep them grounded and balanced is a huge problem.

I know from personal experience that what you see and hear can affect your perspective about life. When I was a teenager, some of my favorite musicians were Ice Cube, Easy E, Tupac, Dr. Dre, Snoop Dog, Notorious B.I.G, and many others. As a result of their negative stories about police, I built up a negative attitude about police. I had never had any personal negative interaction with police; however, I had been brainwashed that all police were crooked and dishonest. This was strange because ever since I was a little kid, I wanted to be a police officer. I had allowed the negative feeling of others to cloud my judgment about an entire population of people.

It culminated when I was seventeen years old, at a local fast food restaurant, and I came in contact with a police officer. A couple of my friends and myself were just sitting out front when the officer approached us. As soon as I saw him getting out of his car, I immediately became agitated and irritated by his mere presence. Once he started to speak and ask us questions, I started giving him attitude. I remember saying to him, "Why are you harassing us?"

This officer, instead of getting angry and being upset, continued to talk to me and answered any questions that I had. So I asked him why *all* police officers are crooks, and his answer shocked me! He said that indeed there are crooked cops; however, there are some police who love people and try to make a difference in the community they work in. I told him that I hated police officers. He asked me why. I said, "Because y'all are dirty." And my friends laughed.

He continued to keep his cool and simply asked me about the personal encounter with police who had led to my opinion of all police. This was when I became dumbfounded. I had no answer to give him because I had never had any negative interaction to support my statement. Before he left, he told me to not let the opinions of others become my own. He challenged me to start thinking for myself and formulate my opinions based on my own interactions with police! He said the only real issue most people had with police was an almost instinctive desire not to submit to authority.

Submission does not mean surrender. When you are submissive to authority figures, we are being obedient, and we will be greatly rewarded. You don't have to agree with authority figures in order to be submissive. This is important because often African American young men believe that they have the right to refuse instructions being given by police. The fact is, they are wrong. They absolutely must comply with officer's command when they are stopped in the streets, if for no other reason than they want to live. Fathers should be teaching their children that you don't argue with police on the street! Whether you are right or wrong, this is not the place to plead your case. The courtroom is where you have the option to give your side of the story and plead your case.

When you are stopped by the police, you should attempt to make the contact as brief as possible. You should avoid any fast or sudden movements. Speak to the officer with the understanding that this is his domain. He is in complete control. Attempt to provide the officer with any information that he is requesting without attitude or resistance. Accept whatever conclusion the encounter comes to on the scene. Being arrested is better than be killed. You can fight an arrest, but you cannot fight being dead. Use your head. Think and live to fight another day.

Obedience is better than sacrifice! When you are obedient, your odds of being proven right rise drastically. Obedience allows for your story to be believed and your voice to be heard. Understand that silence is golden. Stop talking and listen God gave you one mouth and two ears for a reason. Attempt to talk less and listen more in every area of your life. Sometimes it is best to just be quite and keep down confusion and frustration.

> The heart of the righteous studies how to answer, but the mouth of the wicked pours forth evil. (Prov. 15:28, NKJV)

Learn to respect the position, if not the person in the position. I cannot stress this enough. You don't have to like the person with authority over you! During interactions with police, understand that you are attempting to make friends. Consider it a business meeting that you want to end as soon as possible! Being submissive means doing what you are asked as long as it does not put you in immediate danger, and it is morally and ethically right.

We can continue to protest and makeup nice quotes for T-shirts. In the meantime, our young men are continuing to be shot dead in the streets without any justification. However, as a man and father, I choose to educate my son about the importance of submitting to authority. Teaching them that whether the officer is right or wrong, they are in control. I have embraced the opportunity and responsibility to ensure that my young African American sons live. Educating my boys that being submissive doesn't cost a thing. Showing them that pride can be detrimental to their lives. Showing them that not to be willing to accept correction can cost them greatly. When you are full of pride, you can not see the forest for the trees. Teaching them that with pride comes a lack of transparency and an unwillingness to admit your mistakes. Success is not possible when you can't be transparent. Finally, being humble and transparent can lead to better outcomes in every phase of life.

Submission Exercises

Scenario number 1: Traffic Stop

You are driving and get pulled over by a police officer! He walks up to your vehicle and says you were speeding. Right before you are stopped, you looked down at the speedometer, and it showed you were going the speed limit! You honestly believe that you were not speeding. How do you handle it?

Scenario number 2: Mistaken Identity

You are shopping in Walmart, and two police officers approach you with the belief that you have been shoplifting. They tell you to walk to the security office with them. You are embarrassed and have not taken anything. How should you handle it?

Scenario number 3: Michael Brown Scenario

You are walking in the middle of the street, and a squad car approaches you and asks you to get on the sidewalk! You feel like the officer is just harassing you! What do you do?

Scenario number 4: Friends to the End

Your best friend has been involved altercation at school. Police are called out, and they are attempting to take your best friend into custody. You get in the way, and a brief verbal altercation ensues between you and the officers. They advise you that if you continue to be combative and argumentative, you will be arrested. What do you do?

Scenario number 5: Park Protector

You are in the park, and you have a licensed registered weapon, and several other park patrons see the weapon and call police. When the police arrived, you are shocked and startled. You know that you are licensed and have done nothing wrong as the officers approach you. What do you do?

7

Purpose for Work

> Hard work spotlights the character of people: some turn up their sleeves, some turn up their noses and some don't turn up at all! (Sam Ewing)
>
> Work is defined as something on which exertion or labor is expended; a task or undertaking. (Dictionary.com)

Why is working important? Working is important because it builds character. Fathers should teach their children that it is important to have a great work ethic. I started working at the tender age of six years old. When I lived in San Francisco, California, my first job was as a break dancer on Fisherman's Warf. When my brother and I would catch the bus and make our way down to the Warf, there were several things that we had to do. First, we knew that we were not allowed to go alone. Second, we developed relationships with people who worked on the Warf so that we had adults that would look out for us in cases of emergency. Third, we knew that we would have to find the materials needed to perform.

So from our very first job, I learned about safety, building relationships, and gathering materials necessary to do my job. Our first job also taught us how to work hard for what we wanted. Coming from a low-income family, break dancing on Fisherman's Warf was one of the only ways that we had to make legal money. However, there were many other young men with the same goal. At times, it could be very competitive trying to find the space to set up and make a living! From that early period, we learned how hard it was to make it in the workplace.

Working at an early age taught us the importance of preservation. Our mother struggled with addiction, so my brother and I would be called on often to buy dinner and pay rent in the hotel room that we lived in. There were times that if we didn't bring any money home, there wouldn't be anything to eat that day. We were making anywhere from $80 to $100 each a day! In the early 1980s, that was a considerable amount of money!

We learned discipline. The discipline to know that it was not anyone else's responsibility to take care of us. We learned that it was our duty to take care of ourselves. Oftentimes, I watch men make excuses as to why they are not where they want to be in life. They blame family, friends, and the system for their problems. Instead of taking the bull by the horns, they expect others to take care of them and get angry when it doesn't happen. They have not come to the realization that it is up to them to sink or swim in the swimming pool of life.

> We were not idle when we were not with you, nor did we eat anyone's food without paying for it. On the contrary, we worked night and day, laboring and toiling so that we would not be a burden to any of you! (2 Thess. 3:7–8, NKJV)

Your willingness to work also shows yours level of commitment to survive and be productive in your community. I can remember the first dollar I ever earned. A stranger walked up to me while I was break dancing and placed that dollar in my hand. I became committed to the cause. Committed to getting up every day and making my way to the Warf so that I could have a little money in my pocket. Committed to becoming self-sufficient, not waiting on any handouts from anyone.

Working builds up pride and self-worth. When I realized I didn't have to depend on others to support me, it gave me a great sense of pride. Having self-worth helped me become confident in my sustainability. I knew that no matter what the circumstance, I would be able to provide for myself and eventually my family.

Working also gave me the ability to have options. Options on where my life would go. The ability to decide who, what, when, and where I was going in the future. It gave me the ability to produce an income for myself. Because I was willing to work, it gave me the ability to save money.

Here are some keys to becoming successful in the workplace. First, be patient. Stop trying to make it to the top overnight. Understand it takes time to receive promotion. It generally takes about five years to become an expert in anything you do. Second, attitudes are important. There is an old statement that says, "Your attitude determines your altitude." And it is such a true statement. The way you carry yourself can either take you to or keep you from your goals and dreams.

Remember, no one wants a negative person around them, so be positive. Third, try not to burn your bridges. You never know where this life may take you. Watch how you talk to your coworkers. Watch what you say about your boss and who you say it too. Fourth, make lasting impressions on those around you. You are powerful so act like it. Its time to step up and show what you are made of and work like your life depends on it.

> Commit your works to the Lord, and your thoughts will be established. (Prov. 16:3, NKJV)

Finding Your Greatness Game

1. Write down three things that concern or interest you.

   _____

   _____

   _____

2. Write down two reasons why this interests you.

   _____

   _____

3. Write down two reasons why you have not pursued these interests.

   _____

   _____

   Working with a integrity and honor will preserve your life! (Ps. 25:21, NKJV)

Are you willing to do the right thing even when no one is watching you? Integrity starts within. What morals and values do you possess? Do you believe in the concept, "Give a man a fish he will eat for a day, teach a man to fish he will eat for a lifetime?" You have an obligation to your children to give a hundred percent while at work. This gives your children the opportunity to see you in a positive light in the workplace. Plus employers value employees who can add value to their company in a respectful manner.

Why is it so important for men to work with integrity? Having integrity helps build trust. When an employer sees that you have integrity, you become a more attractive option for promotion. You want to make your employer feel that you are an asset to the organization. When you are viewed as an asset, it makes it more difficult for employer to let you go.

Men in many cases don't understand that the type of work ethic they display is passed down from generation to generation. When you take pride in your work, it gives a blueprint for your children to follow. I watched my grandfather get up every morning rain, sleet, or snow, and go to work. He never complained about taking care of his grandchildren; he just made it happen.

After retiring from a meat packing plant, he became a taxicab owner/operator! He would leave the house every morning at around 5:00 a.m .and would not return until about 6:00 p.m. for six days a week. His determination had a profound impact on me. His work ethic paves the way for how I would later work to provide for my family. He never called off sick and always made sure the bills were paid.

I was blessed to see my grandfather work with a spirit of excellence for years. I watched him work up until he died! He was the sole provider in the household, making sure he met every need in the home. While working, he received several accolades from the taxicab company for his professionalism in dealing with the public.

What type of work ethic do you have? Are you willing to work hard today so that you can be celebrated tomorrow? If you said yes, then chances are, you are on the right track to a having a spirit of excellence. A spirit that one day will hopefully be inherited by your children. A lasting legacy of not only hard work but integrity in the workplace.

How do I gain integrity and excellence in my life? Seek out smart and wise people to guide you. Bring people into your lives who add value and direction. Remember, people before you have already knocked down doors for you.

> Blessed is the man who walks not in the counsel of the ungodly. (Ps. 1:1, NKJV)

People of great integrity have family fortune. If you are willing to work hard, you will leave a good name for your children. Your children see the value of hard work, and they will adapt your work ethic. Finally, you will leave a legacy of hard work and integrity that continues in your bloodline.

> The just man walks in his integrity; his children are blessed after him. (Prov. 20:7, NKJV)

What does a spirit of excellence look like? It looks like a person willing to do whatever is necessary for the greater good. Having a yes-I-can mindset! Believe that you have the answers to any problems that arise. Have a desire to get the job done no matter what obstacles may come up. The ability to block out any outside distractions and focus on the task at hand.

Integrity Questions

1. Where does integrity start?_____

2. How should be a child's first teacher about the importance of integrity? _____
   _____

3. What is the benefit of having integrity in life?
   _____

4. How do you gain integrity? _____
   _____

5. Why is it important for fathers to have good work ethic? _____

6. Fill in the blanks: If you give a man a _____, he will eat for a day; however, if you _____ a man how to fish, he will eat for a _____!

8

Don't Be Lazy!

> Time management is an essential part of becoming gainfully and successfully employed! (Dictionary.com)

During my time in the United States Army, I learned the value of time management. During basic training, we would have to get up at 4:00 a. m. to do physical training. By 6:00 a.m., we were back preparing for breakfast and getting ready to clean the barracks. Once we got up we would be gone away from our beds until about 8:00 p.m. During this period, I learned that time is the only commodity that we can't get back; once it's gone, it's gone. Only successful people understand the importance of time and how to use it to your advantage in both work and life. Fathers, teaching your children about time management can keep them focused on their goals and help them avoid wasting time on the road to success.

Those who are willing to manage their time wisely will be greatly rewarded for their actions. They understand that hard work pays off. They not only work hard, they work diligently as well.

When I think of hard work paying off, I'm reminded of the man who had a dream of becoming a great motivational speaker. He had no formal training. All he knew was that he had a dynamic story to tell. When he told his family members about his dream, they told him he was crazy. They said that dreams don't pay, and they encouraged him to stay on his job, making a decent salary with decent benefits. At first, he listened to them, but he continued to have this burning desire that would not go away that he was destined to be a great motivational speaker.

His dream was to change lives with his story of perseverance and strength. So a few years later, he went to a couple of friends whom he had known for years, and he shared his desire to become a motivational speaker, and they laughed at him and said, "You have a great story, but it won't pay your bills." He had eight more years to retirement, and they encouraged him that he should stay focused on making it to retirement.

After a couple more years of putting his dreams on the back burner, he finally decided that he could wait no longer. He quit his job and followed his dream to motivate and encourage others. At first, things started off slow, and he was barely getting by. However, after a few months, he started getting calls from churches, civic groups, and eventually, the business community all willing to pay for his services. He delivered his messages with so much passion and energy he became a hot commodity in the world of motivational speakers. Groups all over the nation began requesting him for speaking engagements. Once he became one of the leading motivational speakers in the country, his family and friends then started to believe in his dream.

He only became successful when he worked with a spirit that was beyond his circumstances. He became consumed with seeing where he wanted to be instead of where he was at that very moment. Finally, he refused to give up on his dream! He realized that if you want to fly, you must first leap. Leap off the cliff of life! Knowing that at first you will fall but eventually, your wings will sprout and you will begin to fly. Later in life, he was asked if he had any regrets. He said the only regret he had in life was the time he wasted in not believing in himself. He realized that his lack of belief in himself and lack of time management slowed the progress to his goals.

> The Diligent find freedom in their work, the lazy are oppressed by work. (Prov. 12:24, NKJV)

Tips to time management

Plan each day! Planning each day can help you accomplish more and feel more in control of your life. Prioritizing your task will ensure that you spend your time and energy on those things that are truly important. Say no to nonessential tasks. Consider your goals and schedule before agreeing to take on additional work. Learn to delegate assignments.

Being on time is to be late; being early is to be on time. You must become a respecter of other people's time. Successful people value their time and your lack of respect for their time is the quickest way to lose their respect. People also don't like to hear excuses about why you are not respecting their work schedule. Being where you are supposed to be when you are supposed to be there. Doing what you are supposed to be doing is what successful people are looking for. Take pride in yourself makes a name for you in life.

Your Attitude About Time Management

1. Do you think that time management is important? _____

2. Are you willing to make a pledge to be on time in the future? _____

3. Do you believe your willingness to be on time have any effect on your employability? _____

4. If you were an employer what type of employee would you hire? One that was always on time or one that had no respect for time! Why?

_____

_____

The Top 10 time wasters are!

1. Telephone interruptions
2. Drop-in visitors
3. Meetings Scheduled and Unscheduled
4. Crises
5. Lack of objectives, priorities, and deadlines
6. Cluttered desk and personal disorganization
7. Ineffective delegation and personal involvement in routine affairs and small details
8. Attempting too much at once
9. Confused chains of authority and responsibility
10. Inadequate, inaccurate, or delayed information

Five Tips to making a schedule

1. Schedule out each hour of your day!
2. Make your schedule flexible!
3. Reserve an hour a day of uncommitted time!
4. Do not neglect your personal life. Build in time for your family!
5. Schedule time to relax among your priorities!

9

ROAR like a Lion!

> Understanding is the first step to acceptance, and only with acceptance can there be recovery! (J. K. Rowling)

I finally get it! For the first time in my life, I can say I truly understand what it means to be a father. What it means to be the leader of my family, to be authoritative, a visionary, and a provider. Now that I have understanding, I promise to step into this role with my whole being! I cannot change my yesterday, but I can make today and tomorrow better. In fact, I'm thankful for my yesterday because it is directly responsible for my tomorrow!

> Life is what happens while you're busy making other plans! (Allen Saunders)

I'm thankful for every struggle I have ever faced in my life. Thankful for every person who doubted I would make it. I am taking all that negative energy and channeling it into positive energy that fuels my fire to be a better man, husband, and father. I refuse to go backward. Through my many struggles, I have found purpose, my reason for being, the *why* for my life. With this newfound purpose and destiny, I will scream from the mountaintops for men and fathers to reconnect with their children because it is written.

> Don't cry because it's over, smile because it happened! (Dr. Seuss)

My life's mission will be to get fathers to see themselves as God sees them in the family structure. To encourage them to not take no for an answer when it comes to relationship with their children! Teach them that their lives have meaning and values so they can in return teach their children the same. I will mentor fathers so that they can mentor their own children. I will show men how to take the mistakes of their past and use them as the gifts of their future.

Learning to ROAR

1. Men shouldn't take _____ for an answer when trying to develop a relationship with their children.

2. Men need to know that they bring _____ to the lives of their children.

3. Your mistakes are valuable _____ to use in helping raise your children.

> A man must be big enough to admit his mistakes, smart enough to profit from them, and strong enough to correct them! (John C. Maxwell)

> Rock bottom became the solid foundation on which I rebuilt my life! (J. K. Rowling)

I am whatever you say I am. I had done so much wrong in my marriage. I was an adulterer. I was physically, emotionally, and verbally abusive, but I refused to let this be what defined me as a man. I needed to take a deeper look at myself and decide how my life would be. I remember a conversation with my ex-wife when she said that I was abusive. She said that there were moments when she was scared of me. For the first time in my life, I was quiet, and I heard her. I looked back on our relationship and realized that it was true. Every word was true about me.

That day, I realized that if I was going to become all that God had designed me to be, I would have to make drastic changes in my life. I started praying daily to overcome the anger that had held me prisoner for all these years. I found scriptures that talked about being angry and how foolish words and actions only created more problems. I read them three times a day until they were ingrained in my spirit. After a while, I realized that because I had made my anger a point of emphasis, my attitude started to change. I became more patient and tolerant of others.

> A fool gives full vent to his anger, but a wise man keeps himself under control! (Prov. 29:11, NKJV)

Even though me and my ex-wife had gone through so much and I realized that we couldn't go forward with the relationship, I still needed to complete my process by admitting my wrongdoing to her. So one day after I had built myself up spiritually, I went to her face to face and said, "Yes, I was an abuser." I apologized and asked for forgiveness. I also realized that by God's strength, I could face the truth of my past so that I could walk confidently into what he had planned for my future.

This seems familiar. When I was a young man, I joined the military. One of the things they did to us when we got to basic training was to take –twenty-five to fifty individuals from different races, nationalities, and socioeconomic backgrounds and turn them into a team. They wanted everyone to think with one mission, one heartbeat, and one mind. In order to do this, they used deprogramming techniques to break us down. We called this having the military mindset.

I think that this exactly the process that I was taken through on a spiritual level in order to become I am today.

A new man with a new mindset and new perspective on life. One who allows me to understand that my mistakes in life were merely my building blocks that would lead me to conquer all my life's obstacles. Allowing me to share my mistakes with others and help prevent them from making the same mistakes.

My life was turned completely upside down. I had to sit in my own mess and find my way back from the brink of destruction. I had to accept responsibility for my actions. I essentially had to do open heart surgery on myself. Mentally, I had to forgive myself for who I had become. I myself had to come to the reality that my heavenly father loves me and wanted me to love me as well. It was necessary for me to be broken so that I could be put back together again even stronger.

> The world as we have created it is a process of our thinking. It cannot be changed without changing our thinking! (Albert Einstein)

It was important to stay busy. Being idle can lead to self-destructive behavior. Keeping positive thoughts and staying about the business of the business was paramount in overcoming the hurdles of divorce. I worked two jobs, ascertained my degree from college, and tried to be an effective parent. At times, it became very difficult trying to balance all phases of my life. If it were not for God and positive people in my life encouraging me along the way, I would not have made it. My friends continued to encourage and motivate me through the tough times, to not give up on my goals and dreams.

Graduation Day 2012

Finally, hard work pays off! Exactly seventeen days before my divorce was to be final, I was scheduled to graduate from Christian Brothers University. On the morning of graduation, I was driving to the ceremony; and as I got close to the school, my favorite songs came on the radio. The song was Marvin Sapp's "Never Would Have Made It." While listening to the song, I just began to cry. I cried because I thought about all the struggles and sacrifices that were made to get me to this day. As I stood among all the other graduates, I couldn't help but to think about the glory behind my story. The fact that I had made it through all these life trials and accomplished a major goal that I set in my life. I learned through it all that I have the power through Christ that strengthens me to overcome any and all situations that I will face in life and become successful.

> Blessed is the man who perseveres under trail, because when he has stood the test, he will receive the crown of life that God has promised to those that love him. (James 1:12, NKJV)

I will not stop until I have started a national fatherhood movement; the likes of which has not been seen since the Civil Rights movement of the 1960s. I believe that fatherlessness is the Civil Rights movement of our day. I pledge to dedicate my life to seeing men restore themselves to the lives of their children.

> A dream doesn't become reality through magic; it takes sweat, determination and hard work! (Colin Powell)

Men ROAR Pledge to Roar Like a Lion!

I pledge to be present for my children! To be an authoritative visionary who provides! I pledge to share my fears, failures, and fortunes! To speak life into my children, I pledge to conquer any anger, disappointment, and resentment that affect my ability to be a good father. My role as a father is pivotal in the development and success of my child. I pledge to restore order, attitudes, and responsibility in myself, my children, and my community. To share the knowledge gained through this program with other young men and help them grow into great men and great fathers.

> I cannot think of any need in childhood as strong as the need for a father's protection! (Sigmund Freud)

Identifying the Man Inside

1. In order to consider yourself a man, you must first conquer _____ and _____!

2. Know that your role as a father is _____ in the development of your child!

3. Be willing to restore _____ attitudes and _____ in _____, my _____, and my _____!

The Rebuilding Process

During the rebuilding process, I learned who I am. I learned that I have the ability to compassionately touch the hearts of people who are hurting. I learned that I am strong, confident, and powerful beyond measure. I learned how to be comfortable in my own skin. I learned that our falls in life are not important; it is how we rise from those falls that will determine our true worth and value to society. I now use it for good! Every experience in life is positive because I choose to use it as such.

What I learned about me is that I am destined for success. My life has equipped me to become all that God has designed me to be! I am mighty! I am resilient! I will succeed in all my future endeavors!

I am better now than I have ever been, and I still have room to develop and growth! I am moving from the foolishness of my youth to the wisdom of my future—from ignorance to intelligence. I understand the responsibility that I have now as a man and father to my family and my community. Because I care about people, I share my story to inspire others! No excuses for my past, just making better decisions in the future. Make the decision to be better and you can. We are cut from the same cloth, and if I can do it, so can you. Just decide. Through it all, I was still a father to my children. I loved them unconditionally and understood that *being present is the most precious, priceless, and perfect gift a father can give his child.*

PART II

WORDS OF LOVE TO MY WIFE AND CHILDREN

10

For That Reason Alone, I Love You

This poem is dedicated to the people I love most in the world—my children. Imani, Marcus, Kyla, Tyler, and Mykaela, I love you guys more than you will ever know. I am so proud of each one of you because despite all my mess, you all are turning out to be everything I asked God for. You all are leaders. You walk to your own drum beat, and I love that about you. Don't ever change. I want to start by saying to you, Imani, I am sorry. Sorry for not being there in your life everyday. It pains me to know that I haven't given you the same time, attention, and love that Marcus, Kyla, Tyler, and Mykaela have gotten. Well, baby, let me tell you that I love you just the same; and I admit I have made mistakes when it comes to our relationship, and for that I apologize. You are my firstborn child, and for that reason alone, you are special in my eyes. I pray daily that our relationship grows and strengthens over time. Marcus, we also have had our battles over the years, but you have never given up on me, and I appreciate that. You are more of a man than I will ever be. Your compassion is a thing of beauty. Your spirit is true. You are not afraid to show your feelings. Don't ever change. You are my only begotten son, and for that reason alone, I love you. Kyla, in the short time I have been in your life, I have watched you blossom from a shy girl into a confident young lady. You have the ability to influence others. Use your gift to help people make positive choices. You have a great sense of humor, great spirit, and I often act like I don't care but I truly do, which is our thing. You are my third daughter, and for that reason alone, I love you! Tyler, we have had our disagreements, but know that I want the best for you. You are an overseer. Use your gift as a protector to help those who are less fortunate. Stand up for those who have no voice in this world. Most importantly, Tyler, believe in yourself. You are my second son, and for that reason alone, I love you. Mykaela, my baby, you are the happiest kid I know. You are growing up, baby, but make sure you keep your essence of happiness, and don't let anyone still your joy in this life. I love that when you look at me, you don't see all my mess. You see your daddy, and no matter what, you love me unconditionally. Mykaela, believe in yourself. You are beautiful, smart, and funny. You are my baby girl, the last born; and for that reason alone, I love you. To my children, I pray that everything your hands touch, God will bless. I pray that in some way, I have been an inspiration to your lives. I ask each of you to do better by your children than I did by you, and if I failed you in any way, forgive me with the love of God. You will learn that on this journey of life, we do the best we can with the knowledge we have. With that being said, children, please gain knowledge in all that you do. Be the best that you can be. Keep God first and stand on his Word for your lives. Show mercy to others whenever possible, and stay humble! For these reasons alone, *I love you*!

11

What Your Love Has Done

Your love rescued me when I was in despair.
You came into my life and showed me that you really care.
The reverence that you showed for me, I felt it in my soul.
And like a watered plant, our love will continuously grow!

Your love and faith helps to recharge my battery.
And with God by our side, we can go as far as our minds can see.
Your belief in me gives me strength to face the road ahead.
With you by my side, we will succeed and live life with no regret!

The new Michelle and Barack who we claim to be!
The next power couple, ready to start our legacy!
Letting nothing stand in our way as we rise to the top!
Simply stated, baby, I thought I told y'all that we won't stop. I thought I told y'all that we won't stop!

Marriage is a spiritual thing, apart of God's great design!
You for me, me for you, our love will stand the test of time!
We will trust in God for all things, both seen and unseen!
Remember this, my love, *loyalty over everything*!
I love you, Latoria Taylor!

Afterword

No work is insignificant. All labor that uplifts humanity has dignity and importance and should be undertaken with painstaking excellence! (Martin Luther King Jr)

Am I really making a difference? is the question I was asking myself. I think anytime we decide that we want to make a lasting impact on humanity, we ask that question. I struggled thinking things were not moving fast enough. Oftentimes, we think, *Hey, I'm doing a good thing so everyone should immediately catch the vision and help make it happen.* I, on many occasions, have contemplated giving up on my dreams to see men and families get healed.

Several months ago, I held a fatherhood conference for young men ages seventeen to twenty-four. The group was from the local job corp; the young men came from many different backgrounds and circumstances. From the first day of the classes, they were skeptical of what this program could offer them. They, however, reluctantly followed along with the requirements of the program. As I talked to them about fatherhood and what a father should be, something happened.

They started to realize that they had been slighted. They began to recognize that fathers are important. I asked each young man about their relationship with their father. A majority of them had a distaste for their fathers because they simply weren't present. Some said if they had the chance to see their fathers, they would want to fight them out of anger over being abandoned.

One young man in particular stood out to me because he looked like Malcolm X. He stood about 6'2" in height, and he had that brownish red hair. His name was Courtney, and when I first met him, he seemed a little shy. He spoke in a very low almost whisper tone. He sat in the back of the class when we began; however by week three, he had made his way to the front of the room. He started asking more and more questions. It seemed that for the first time in his life, he had been placed in an environment that allowed him the opportunity to learn from a man about manhood.

One week, I told the young men that near the end of class, I would give them a chance to tell their story. Several young men got up and told everyone how they had been mistreated or mislead by their fathers. When it was Courtney's turn, he got up and started talking in that same low tone voice we had heard from the beginning of the classes. We could barely hear or understand his speaking. However, the more he talked, the more confident he seemed to appear. He told us that he lost his mother in 2012, and that he never had a relationship with his father.

He said he was an angry child when his mother passed, and he never really knew why. He told the group that the past several weeks, he has learned a lot about life, purpose, and forgiveness. We watched Courtney's demeanor change completely before our eyes! It appeared that a weight had been lifted from his shoulder. He stood there confident and said that he wanted to become a motivational speaker and share his story with people who have lost loved ones. Through his own pain, he has found a purpose that can impact the lives of many. What he didn't realize was that his freedom encouraged me to continue in my mission to change lives.

For anyone who has ever questioned their call to change lives, questioned the impact they could make, questioned if they could do it—yes, you can because you are important! You have what it takes. Your story can help. Your misery can become your ministry. There are people you have never met, *waiting on you* to get your life together, so that you can *save* their lives! Simply stated, *you matter*!

References

Here's how each entry should be formatted:

- The elements are separated by periods rather than by commas.
- The facts of publication are not enclosed in parentheses.
- The first-listed author's name, according to which the entry is alphabetized and usually inverted (last name first).
- The date should be placed directly after the author's name.
- As in a note, titles are capitalized headline-style unless they are in a foreign language.
- Titles of larger works (e.g., books and journals) are italicized, and titles of smaller works (e.g., chapters, articles) or unpublished works are presented in roman and enclosed in quotation marks.

- Noun forms such as *editor*, *translator*, *volume*, and *edition* are abbreviated, but verb forms such as *edited by* and *translated by*—abbreviated in a note—are spelled out.

Use the two examples below as a guide in revising your list:

Albiston, Catherine R. 2005. "Bargaining in the Shadow of Social Institutions: Competing Discourses and Social Change in the Workplace Mobilization of Civil Rights." *Law and Society Review* 39 (1): 11–47.

Moynihan, Daniel P. *The Negro Family: The Case for National Action*. 1965.

Anderson, A. C. "Quote by AC Anderson: 'You Are the Only Common Denominator in Everyth...'." Goodreads. Accessed January 20, 2015. http://www.goodreads.com/quotes/1119765-you-are-the-only-common-denominator-in-everything-that.

Anderson, K. 2013. "The Number of U.S. Children Living in Single Parent Homes Is Nearly Doubled in 50 Years." *Census Data: Life Site News*.

McKay, Brett, and Kay McKay. "Benjamin Franklin's Virtuous Life: The Virtue of Humility." The Art of Manliness. Accessed May 28, 2015. http://www.artofmanliness.com/2008/05/25/the-virtuous-life-humility/.

Bancroft, Lundy. "When Dad Hurts Mom: Helping Your Children Heal the Wounds of Witnessing Abuse." Domesticviolenceroundtable.org. Accessed September 1, 2015.

http://www.domesticviolenceroundtable.org/effectsonchildren.

Bronislaw Malinowski. 2014. "The Negro Family:The Case for National Action. n.d. In Wikipedia Retrieved December 12,

http://www.enwikipedia.org/wiki/The Negro Family.

Edmund Burke. 2015. "goodreads.com. n.d. In Goodreads Retrieved January 20,

http://www.goodreads.com/quotes/111024-those-whodon-t-know-history-are-doomed-to-repeat-it

BV. Brown PH.D.; S. Bzostek. 2003."Violence in the Lives of Children."

https://www.ncjrs.gov/App/Publication/abstract.aspx?ID=203660

Chicago Tribune. 2012. "A better system for child support: A switch to income share makes sense." articles.chicagotribune.com January 16, http://articles.chicagotribune.com/2012-01-16/opinion/ct-editsupport-20120116_1_child-support-services-parentsjoan-colen.

Crick, N. R., & Grotpeter, J. K. 1995. Relational aggression, gender, and Social-psychological adjustment. Child

Development, 66, 710-722.

Criss Jami. 2015 "goodreads.com. n.d. In Goodreads Retrieved January 20,

http://www.goodreads.com/quotes/512034-to-shareyour-weakness-is-to-make-yourself-vulnerable-to

Cosby, Bill. 2015. "BrainyQuote.com. Xplore Inc, 2015.

http://www.brainyquote.com/qoutes/quotes/b/billcosby386254.html

Davidson, Andrew. 2015. "goodreads.com. n.d. In Goodreads Retrieved January 20

http://www.goodreads.com/quotes/961601-i-am-morethan-my-scars

Dollar, Dr. Creflo. Dollar, Taffi L. 2002. "The Successful Family. Everything You need to know to build a stronger family." College Park: Creflo Dollar Ministries, 235-238. Print

Dollar, Dr. Creflo. Dollar, Taffi L. 2002. "The Successful Family. Everything You need to know to build a stronger family." College Park: Creflo Dollar Ministries, 2002. 348. Print

http://www.goodreads.com/quotes/111024-those-who-don-t-know-history-are-doomed-to-repeat-it

Domestic Violence Statistics Staff. "Domestic Violence Statistics." domesticviolencestatistics.org. 2015.

Domestic Violence Statistics for Medical and Educational Research (DVSMER). 23 January 2015 <

Durant, Will. 2015. "quoteland.com. n.d. In qouteland Retrieved January 20,

http://www.goodreads.com/quotes/562457-so-the-storyof-man-runs-in-a-dreary-circle

Einstein, Albert. 2015. "goodreads.com n.d. In Goodreads Retrieved January 20,

http://www.goodreads.com/quotes/1799-the-world-aswe-have-created-it-is-a-process

Einstein, Albert. 2015. "goodreads.com n.d. In Goodreads Retrieved January 20, http://www.goodreads.com/quotes/1799-the-world-aswe-have-created-it-is-a-process

Ewing, Sam. 2015. "goodreads.com n.d. In Goodreads Retrieved January 20,

http://www.goodreads.com/author/quotes/1662464.Sam_Ewing

Fox, Jim. 2003. "quoteland.com. June 21,

http://forum.quoteland.com/eve/forums/a/tpc/f/99191541/m/9131971956

Freud, Sigmund. 2015. "BrainyQuote.com. Xplore Inc,

http://www.brainyquote.com/quotes/quotes/s/sigmundfre138674.htm

Harper, Cynthia C. and McLanahan, Sara S. 2004. " Father Absence and Youth Incarceration." Journal of Research on Adolescence 14 September: 369-397.

Joyce, James. 2015 "entheos.com. n.d. In entheos Retrieved January 20,

https://www.entheos.com/quotes/by_topic/soul

King Jr, Martin Luther. 2015. "goodreads.com n.d. In Goodreads Retrieved January 20, http://www.goodreads.com/quotes/30178-no-work-isinsignificant-all-labor-that-uplifts-humanity-has

Maxwell, John C. "goodreads.com n.d. In Goodreads Retrieved January 20,

http://www.goodreads.com/author/quotes/68.John_C_Maxwell

Mayo Clinic Staff. "Disease and Conditions. "Oppositional defiant disorder (ODD)." MayoClinic.com. 2014. November 25, Mayo Foundation for Medical Education and Research (MFMER). 22 Jan 2015 <

http://www.mayoclinic.org/diseases-conditions/oppositional-defiant-disorder/basics/symptoms/con-20024559

Miller, Henry. 2015. "goodreads.com n.d. In Goodreads Retrieved January 20,

http://www.goodreads.com/quotes/112213-true-strengthlies-in-submission-which-permits-one-to-dedicate

Norman, Danielle. 2015. The "I Don't Need A Man" Epidemic." Retrieved February 9,

http://www.yourtango.com/201176724/i-don-t-need-man-epidemic

Osborne, C., & McLanahan, S. 2007. "Partnership instability and child well-being." Journal of Marriage and Family, 69, 1065-1083

Parenting. 2015. "Action Plan for Rebuilding Relationships with Your Children." drphil.com Retrieved January 31, 2015

http://www.drphil.com/articles/article/537

Parenting 101: 2010. Responsibility and Accountability. "examiner.com." August 7,

http://www.examiner.com/article/parenting-101-responsibility-and-accountability

Powell, Colin. 2015. "goodreads.com n.d. In Goodreads Retrieved January 20

http://www.goodreads.com/quotes/313423-a-dreamdoesn-t-become-reality-through-magic-it-takes-sweat

Ramsey, Dave. 2015. "BrainyQuote.com. Xplore Inc,

http://www.brainyquote.com/quotes/keywords/financial.html

Rawlings, J.K. 2015. "goodreads.com n.d. In Goodreads Retrieved January 20, http://www.goodreads.com/quotes/67454-understandingis-the-first-step-to-acceptance-and-only-with

Rawlings, J.K. 2015. "goodreads.com n.d. In Goodreads Retrieved January 20,

http://www.goodreads.com/quotes/396385-and-so-rockbottom-became-the-solid-foundation-on-which

Rawlings, J.K. 2015. "goodreads.com n.d. In Goodreads Retrieved January 20,

http://www.goodreads.com/quotes/396385-and-so-rockbottom-became-the-solid-foundation-on-which

Richmond, Michael II. 2012. "The Spirit Behind The Music. Exposing the hidden agenda to distort the minds of today's generation." Memphis: Understanding for Life

Ministries, 4. Print.

Richmond, Michael II. 2012. "The Spirit Behind The Music. Exposing the hidden agenda to distort the minds of today's generation." Memphis: Understanding for Life

Ministries, 2012. 20-21. Print

Saunders, Allen. 2015. "goodreads.com n.d. In Goodreads Retrieved January 20, http://www.goodreads.com/quotes/467-life-is-whathappens-to-you-while-you-re-busy-making

SooHoo, S. 2009. Examining the invisibility of girl-to-girl bullying in schools: A call to action. International Electronic Journal For Leadership in Learning, 13(6). Retrieved from:

http://www.eric.ed.gov/PDFS/EJ940628.pdf on January 24, 2015

Suess, Dr. 2015. "goodreads.com n.d. In Goodreads Retrieved January 20, 2015

http://www.goodreads.com/quotes/1173-don-t-crybecause-it-s-over-smile-because-it-happened

Work. 2015. "dictionary.com Unabridged. Random House, Inc. January 21, <dictionary.com

http://dictionary.reference.com/browse/work>

Taylor, Meiangelo. 2012. "Men Restoring Order Attitudes and Responsibility." Unpublished

The Holy Bible, New King James Version. Nashville: Thomas Nelson, 1982. Print.

Time-management. 2015. "dictionary.com Unabridged. Random House, Inc January 21, <dictionary.com

http://dictionary.reference.com/browse/time%20management?s=t

US Census Bureau. 2011. "Children's Living Arrangements and Characteristics: March, Table C8. Washington D.C."

Victor, Delvin. 2015. "GoodReads.com. n.d. In Goodreads Retrieved January 20,

http://www.goodreads.com/quotes/tag/fatherhood

Warren, Roland C. 2014. "The Absent Father." November 10, 2014

https://makupsy.wordpress.com/2014/11/10/the-absent-father/